# POWERFUL!!    DEFINITIVE!!    VALUABLE!!

## PRAISE FOR JOHN ELMORE

*"Few books say it better or simpler than this one.* Fighting For Your Life *uncomplicates how African-Americans must deal with a bias criminal justice system. I was inspired by John Elmore's wisdom, insight and willingness to share critical information that most would have to pay for in either time or money. This book is a must read for all those who are serious about avoiding the pitfalls, tricks and misconduct of America's criminal justice system. My hat goes off to John Elmore for such an important contribution to our community".*

—George C. Fraser, **Author;** *Success Runs In Our Race* and *Race For Success*

*An essential reference for those facing imprisonment. Attorney Elmore offers, in layman's terms, **everything you need to know about the criminal justice system.***

—Ann Burns, Editor, *Library Journal*

*An unfortunate aspect of life in America is that young black men are very likely to have a run-in with the law.* **Fighting for Your Life** *tells you in simple language how to protect your rights."*

—Melvin B. Miller, Attorney, Director of One Unity Bank

*"This book is necessary...because if we don't give our kids time, the system will."*

—Terrie M. Williams, Founder and President of The Stay Strong Foundation

# FIGHTING FOR YOUR LIFE:

## The African-American Criminal Justice Survival Guide

John V. Elmore

Edited by Yvonne Rose

Amber Books

Phoenix
New York      Los Angeles

First Edition
*Fighting For Your Life: The African-American Criminal Justice Survival* Guide

By John V. Elmore
Edited by Yvonne Rose

Published by:
**Amber Books**
A Division of Amber Communications Group, Inc.
1334 East Chandler Boulevard, Suite 5-D67
Phoenix, AZ 85048
amberbk@aol.com
WWW.AMBERBOOKS.COM

Tony Rose, Publisher/Editorial Director    Samuel P. Peabody, Associate Publisher
John V. Elmore, Esq., Co-Publisher    Yvonne Rose, Senior Editor
The Printed Page, Interior & Cover Design    Wayne Summerlin, Author Photos

ISBN#: 0-9727519-3-9

Library of Congress Cataloging-in-Publication Data
Elmore, John V., 1956-
    Fighting for your life : the African-American criminal justice
survival guide / by John V. Elmore ; edited by Yvonne Rose.-- 1st ed.
      p. cm.
Includes index.
ISBN 0-9727519-3-9
    1. Criminal justice, Administration of--United States. 2. Discrimination
in criminal justice administration--United States. 3. Attorney and client--United States.
4. African American criminals. 5. African American youth. I. Rose, Yvonne. II. Title.

KF9223.E438 2004
364.973'0896'073—dc22

        2004042200

# Contents

# Dedication

*This book is dedicated to all those victims
of our American society who have, for centuries,
been wrongfully charged, incarcerated, or executed…
because of the color of their skin….and to their parents,
grandparents, husbands, wives, brothers, sisters, aunts,
uncles, cousins, children and unborn babies
who suffer the consequences of those injustices.*

# Acknowledgments

I stand on the shoulders of those who came before me. This book is the result of the character and work ethic that my parents Lorna R. Elmore and Herbert V. Elmore instilled in me. To my parents I am eternally grateful.

To my wife Redahlia, thank you for your love, motivation and prayer about this book as it progressed.

To my late grandparents, uncles, aunts, my brother and sister, my brothers and sister-in-law, nephews and nieces, cousins and other family members, thank you for your love support and encouragement in all that I do.

Without the help of my editor and publisher Yvonne and Tony Rose this book would not have been possible. The Roses with Amber Books are pioneers in publishing self-help books for African-Americans. I am proud to have the opportunity to join their mission.

Special thanks to my Aunt Madeline Scott whose appropriate blend of enthusiasm and criticism strengthened the book.

To author Terrie Williams who prophetically told me that there is a book inside of me gave me guidance, thank you for all your support.

Thanks also to Mason Ash, Jennifer Parker, Stephan Perry, Rev. Arthur Boyd, Rev. Troy Bronner, Rev. Richard Stenhouse, Rev. Darius Pridgen, Nicholas Hicks, David Feldman, Ayoka Tucker, Donald Silverberg, Rev. Leeland James, Jonathan K. Lee, Kenneth Nixon, my legal staff, the members of Bethel AME Church, The members of Elim Christian Fellowship Church, Frank Mesiah, the Buffalo Chapter of the N.A.A.C.P., The brothers of Omega Psi Phi Fraternity, Lisa Rodwin, The Black Capital Network, my friends at GiGi's Restaurant, the Riggins Family, Rocky Ephraim, Philip Regan, Dan Herbeck, Lou Michel, Pamela Hayes, Lee Coppola, members of the Erie County Bar Association, members of the Minority Bar Association, Randall F. Innis, Esq., Daniel Barry, Micky Howard, Buffalo City Court Judge E. Jeanette Ogden, Shawn Fagan, Fran Mesiah, Craig Hannah, Esq., Sharon West, Terry McKelvey, Esq., Members of the Links, Inc., *The Buffalo Challenger*, *The Buffalo Criterion*, and *The Buffalo News*.

To my clients who have trusted me for the past nineteen years in the fight for their lives, I thank you for your faith.

To my children Sonya, Twila, Justin and Kristen, I love you and am very proud of you. I expect nothing in return for the things that I have done for you except the expectation that you enjoy life and continue to be good people. Remember that it takes a lifetime to earn a good reputation and only a single indiscretion to ruin it.

—John V. Elmore, Esq.

# About the Author

John Elmore is a practicing criminal defense attorney with offices in Buffalo and Niagara Falls, New York. He was co-counsel with Attorney James Harrington in Western New York's first Death penalty case in forty years. Their efforts resulted in a life sentence for Jonathan Parker, who was convicted in the shooting of Buffalo Police Officer Charles McDougald. Mr. Elmore is a former New York State Trooper, Manhattan Assistant District Attorney and New York State Assistant Attorney General. He has taught Criminal Justice Administration at Buffalo State College and Medaille College. Mr. Elmore has also lectured at various Continuing Legal Education seminars sponsored by the New York State Capital Defender's Office, the Erie County Bar Association and the New York State Bar Association.

The Williamsville resident is a native of Olean, New York. He is a member of the Olean High School Athletic Hall of Fame. He was the Captain of the track team at Mansfield University, where he received a Bachelor of Arts Degree in Criminal Justice Administration. A 1984 graduate of Syracuse University College of Law, Attorney John Elmore is past president of the Minority Bar Association of Western New York, serves on the Erie County Bar Association Judiciary Ratings and nominating committees, and is a member of the National Association of Criminal Defense Attorneys. He is also a member of the New York State Association of Criminal Defense Attorneys and the New York State Defenders Association.

As a life member of the NAACP, John Elmore has served as a past board member and volunteer attorney for the Buffalo Branch for ten years. He is a past board member of the William-Emslie YMCA and has been a board member, coach and sponsor for the Kensington-Bailey Little League. Mr. Elmore has sponsored youth teams in the

Niagara Falls Boys Club and Gloria J. Parks Community Center. He is a participant in the Omega Psi Phi Fraternity mentoring program and the Elim Christian Fellowship Church Rites of Passage Program. His dedication to youth was highlighted when he was presented with the Parent's Magazine "Good Neighbor Award" and the Buffalo News Citizen of the Year Award.

Mr. Elmore is also a recipient of the Buffalo Chapter of the NAACP Medgar Evers Civil Rights Award and the Erie County Bar Association Criminal Justice Award.

# About the Editor

Yvonne Rose is the Vice President and Senior Editor of Amber Communications Group, Inc. The Company's imprints include: Amber, Busta, Colossus, Ambrosia, Amber/Wiley Books.

AMBER BOOKS, is the nation's largest African-American self-help and career guide book publishing house and the recipient of the Chicago Black Book Fair and Conference Independent Publisher/Press Award of the Year, as well as the 2003 BlackBoard BestSeller's African-American Publisher of the Year Award.

Yvonne has served as editor and co-editor of the entire Amber Communications Group, Inc. catalogue, including: *Fighting for Your Life: The African-American Criminal Justice Survival Guide; Urban Suicide: The Enemy We Choose Not to See, The African-American Teenager's Guide to Personal Growth, Health, Safety, Sex and Survival; 101 Real Money Questions—The African-American Financial Question and Answer Book; Beautiful Black Hair; The Afrocentric Bride—A Styling Guide; Born Beautiful—The African-American Teenager's Complete Beauty Guide, The African-American Woman's Guide to Great Sex, Happiness, and Marital Bliss, The House that Jack Built: The Autobiography of a Successful American Dreamer, Businessman, and Entertainer,* and *Wake Up and Smell the Dollars! Whose Inner City is This Anyway!*

Ms. Rose is also the co-author of the Company's flagship title *Is Modeling for You? The Handbook and Guide for the Young Aspiring Black Model*....a national bestseller.

Prior to entering the book publishing industry, Ms. Rose worked as a writer, publicist, fashion and beauty editor for several national magazines, including: *Sophisticate's Black Hair Care, Unique Hair and Beauty, Black Elegance* and *CLASS*.

Yvonne Rose is also an award-winning journalist with features appearing in *Kip's Business Report, Network Journal* and *Harlem News*.

# Foreword

I am a product of the criminal justice system. Two of my four sons are caught up in the criminal justice system.

One son worked himself from doing one month, to three months, to six months, to one year, to three and a half years, to eight and a half years to life, under New York State's Three Strikes Law, which gives three time offenders life imprisonment. He has been incarcerated in New York State now for thirteen years straight...all his young life wasted. On January 26, 2004 his parole was rejected; he is up again for parole on January 26, 2006.

The other son, through being in the wrong place at the wrong time and using bad judgment, lost a promising football scholarship. He was captain of his team and missed graduating from a prestigious school he'd been attending since first grade. We were able to save him from a three and a half to five year sentence, but with probation and a lifetime stipulation. His life has changed forever.

I was born and raised in the criminal justice system. My father was a heroin drug-user who spent thirty years of his adult life in and out of the criminal justice system. He was a gangster, pimp, hustler...an out-and-out criminal. He finally straightened up in his last twenty years. I loved him very much and buried him, as he wanted, strapped and ready.

My stepfather spent fifteen years in the criminal justice system for killing a man when he was nineteen. When I was twelve, he was released from prison, called my grandmother (my mother was his last girlfriend before prison), came over, and moved into our little project apartment. He was, in some ways, a good man; but, with incarceration, institutionalization, drugs and medications, he was a ruined man. I was finally able to get him out of my mother's life fifteen years later.

My uncle was involved in a massive manhunt and shootout with the Boston Police. After shooting and wounding a policeman, he tried to take his own life, and served fifteen years in prison…blind. My mother's family never, ever recovered from that trauma in their lives. He ruined himself and ruined them…forever.

I'm sure you can see, by now, that I could go on and on…

I was raised in prison. The Whittier Street Housing Projects in Boston were run by former, or soon to be, inmates of the Massachusetts State Prison and Criminal Justice System. Everybody I knew had been in prison or was going to prison, men and women…boys and girls. Rape, robbery, insanity, death, drugs and murder were a normal part of life. I have no childhood friends from that project, from that time, because they either died in prison, still are in prison, were killed committing a felony, died as victims, or are outside still living in prison in their minds.

I, myself, have been jailed. I was in gangs as a teenager, lived in the ghetto and did stupid things, little things that would get me jailed here and there. My father was actually proud of me and began grooming and instructing me for "The Life". Of course, I was jailed, it was all I knew and somehow it seemed right. My longest stretch was a week in the Los Angeles County Jail Criminal Justice System, when I was in my early twenties, for a DWI and traffic infractions. I plead hard before the judge, explained where I had come from, what had brought me to Los Angeles, and where I was going. I plead hard, but I never plead guilty…my father had taught me that. I was released, went to my apartment, moved, leaving no forwarding addresses, and never went back to jail again.

What I had finally realized was that in jail, and this was important…real important…there were no girls!! You couldn't dress right, and the food and the smells were horrific. And, let's not forget those guards. They are your keepers; they own you in the criminal justice system.

As the publisher, I dedicate this book to those people who live in the real ghetto, in a bad environment, in bad conditions, with bad parents, bad schools, drugs, gangs, vermin, roaches, crazy people, f—d-up s—t all around them, and still try every day to stay to the right, to every day fight for their lives!… to every day fight for their lives!…to everyday fight for their lives! This book is dedicated to you…you can make it!

To Yvonne Rose, Amber Books Vice President and Senior Editor who brought the idea to Amber Books, and because she knew how important this book would be for *You,* edited and handled this project with care, love, professionalism and great passion. Thank you. You made this work.

To my Associate Publisher, Samuel P. Peabody, who always believes that we are great and says that we are great.

And, finally to John V. Elmore who has seen you and your child under the most terrifying conditions, and fought for your rights, the rights of the victim and the defendant, all his adult life. For caring and believing in us enough to write what I consider to be **THE MOST IMPORTANT BOOK FOR AFRICAN-AMERICANS WRITTEN IN THE LAST THIRTY YEARS.**

If you don't believe me, just ask the millions of African-American men, women and children, whole generations incarcerated justly and unjustly in the United States of America. If you don't believe me, just ask those unborn children, or those children born living with no father, fathers in jail or f—d up out of jail fathers…just ask them.

And, if you see me and want to talk, I'll tell you more; but here's what I'll tell you now. Trust in God…and Stay to the right. It might be the hardest road, but it's always the best road…and always…always… **FIGHT FOR YOUR LIFE.**

Tony Rose, Publisher/CEO
Amber Communications Group, Inc.
WWW.AMBERBOOKS.COM

*"The most important question in the world is, 'Why is the child crying?'."*
—Alice Walker

# Introduction

As a Defense Attorney, I spend a lot of time counseling young African-American men and women about making better lives for themselves and avoiding lives of crime. Many that I have spoken to are doing very well in life. One of my former clients is now a law school graduate and practicing criminal defense attorney. However, some of the young people have engaged in progressively worse behavior and are now either serving long prison terms or dead. This has been very disheartening. I have also witnessed many young black men and women, who have been wrongfully accused and convicted of crimes because they did not understand the system and lacked the tools to survive it.

One day, I felt the urgent need to write a book about the growing rate of incarceration of African-Americans. In a single day, I went to court on two separate cases for two young men who went to jail. The first, whom I'll call "Eric", had a Federal drug conspiracy case; I represented him for three years, during which time I convinced him to attend college. He did very well at a local community college, the thought of which had never entered his mind until he and I had a long talk and I was able to make him understand that he could lead a very happy and productive life.

Eric's involvement in narcotics started when a major drug dealer recruited him to count money—sometimes $100,000.00 or more, at one time. Eventually, his involvement with the dealer increased; and he was caught delivering a kilo of cocaine to an undercover police informant. He was facing 25 years in a Federal prison; I worked out a plea agreement where he would serve less than four years in prison.

After Eric's sentencing, I spoke with his parents, who thanked me for the good work that I had done on their son's behalf. His father then told me that the major drug dealer and I were the only two men his son had ever looked up to. The drug dealer was dead, having been executed in a turf war. He had asked me to visit Eric in jail: I was needed to keep his son going in a positive direction.

When I left Federal Court, I went to State Court where 18-year old "James" was to be sentenced for a probation violation. James' parents were divorced. His father was unemployed and addicted to crack cocaine; his mother was a devout Christian and employed by a computer company. Unfortunately, when James was young, the courts placed him in the care of his father, who forced him to sell crack. His drug dealing caused problems with other drug dealers in the neighborhood and their house was firebombed. James often ran home through back yards as his gun-toting enemies chased him; numerous times, he heard bullets whistling past his head.

For protection, James bought a gun. I represented him on the gun case and convinced the judge to give him probation. He was arrested again for being in a stolen car. His probation had been violated; and, shortly after turning 18, he was sent to jail for a year. Just before the guards led him away, he cried to his mother that this would never have happened if he had a father like me.

It hurts me to see so many of our young African-American men going to jail instead of college. Many go to jail, having been wrongfully convicted of crimes that they did not commit. Others will go to jail because of a lack of economic opportunities; and others go to jail simply because they did not have someone to show them a better way.

I hope this book will serve as a tool to wake up and fight to save the lives of the next generation of African-American young people, so that they will avoid the criminal justice system. I hope it will educate you and your loved ones about the system and help you make intelligent decisions about the way you conduct your lives.

*"Law and order exist for the purpose of establishing justice and... when they fail in this purpose they become the dangerously structured dams that block the flow of social progress."*
—Reverend Dr. Martin Luther King, Jr.

## Chapter One
# You, Your Attorney and Your Fight For Justice

Unfortunately, thousands of African-American people have been wrongly incarcerated over the years because of rogue cops, shabby lab work and overzealous prosecutors. Being Black in America is a constant "fight for justice."

### Discrimination

The incidents mentioned here are just a few of the many injustices that have been committed by the legal system, against the African-American male, in particular. Typically, the moment a minority group member enters the criminal justice system, that person is at a disadvantage because they don't understand the system. The responsibility of prosecutors and police authorities is to protect the public from those who commit crimes and the innocent from unwarranted prosecution. Their obligation to the public is to see that justice is served in every case.

Data compiled in a new study "Cell Blocks or Classrooms?" reports that while 603,000 African-American men were in college in 2001,

791,000 were imprisoned. The Justice Policy Institute conducted the study, which also found that one out of three African-American men is under the control of the Criminal Justice System. Incarceration costs a state between $20,000 to $30,000 per year, per inmate (*Global Black News*, October 11, 2002 – Cliff Hocker)

▼ 4810 African-American males per 100,000 are incarcerated, compared to 649 per 100,000 white males.

▼ The incarceration rate for African-American females is also high at 349 per 100,000 compared to 68 per 100,000 for white women.

▼ One in eight black males aged 25-29 were in prison or jail at mid-year 2002 and ONE in sixty-three white males in the same age group.

▼ Black males have a 29% chance of serving time in prison at some point in their lives. White males have a 4% chance.

In July 2003 twelve men and women were freed from prison after serving as many as four years in prison on bogus drug-selling charges. In all, 38 African-American people in the town of Tulia, Texas were jailed because of the testimony of an undercover investigator found to have lied repeatedly on the witness stand. A special investigation ordered by a Texas appeals court had determined that the district attorney knew the cop was lying—and did nothing about it. (Source: *USA Today* – July 14, 2003)

A recent nationwide study by the Center for Public Integrity, an ethics watchdog, found more than 2,000 cases over the past three decades in which convictions were overturned or reduced because of abuses by state and local prosecutors.

A prime example of discrimination (or racial profiling), which is too often overlooked, is being in the wrong place at the wrong time. For example, on a recent night—53 people were arrested and 50 were black. Never underestimate the extent of damage or the many consequences that can occur, beginning with your arrest, based on mistaken identity or simply association with a suspect.

One of my clients, wrongfully accused of rape, spent two weeks in jail and lost jobs, the respect of friends in the community, and his girl-friend's affections based only on the claims of the victim to the police. Genetic tests proved that the former high school football star did not rape a 15-year-old girl. I had my client agree to take a DNA test, which proved his innocence and resulted in a dismissal of the charges. Upon his release, my client commented that he felt vindicated; but the system works only if you have a good lawyer.

## Your Legal Advisor—Public Defender or Attorney-for-Hire

Sooner or later almost everyone will need an Attorney. In addition to the traditional "general attorney" who provides a broad scope of services, today you'll find many who specialize in such areas as: Adoption and Family Law; Bankruptcy and Debtor Relief; Civil Law; Criminal Law; or Corporate Law. For instance, in minor criminal cases, a general attorney might be fine; but if your need requires specific knowledge and experience, an attorney who specializes in criminal law will be your best choice. Check with the bar organization in your state to find out what specializations they recognize and how attorneys qualify for those specializations.

## FYI...Legal Resources

*Here are some other sources for finding a lawyer before you need one:*
▼ *Ask for recommendations from friends, associates or community programs*
▼ *Call local Referral Services that have attorney listings*
▼ *Contact your local Bar Association and ask for a list of attorneys in good standing that are experienced in criminal law.*
▼ *Look in the Yellow Pages – Call, interview, get references and fees.*
▼ *News Reports – Listen to your local news to see who's winning cases.*
▼ *Law School Programs – Call the universities in your area for legal programs and services.*

Always interview before you hire. Be sure you like the lawyer and feel comfortable with him or her. Give respect and expect respect in return. During the interview process, ask your lawyer about his or her training and experience in criminal law. If the attorney is a former prosecutor or public defender, he probably has adequate training in criminal law.

You may not consider maintaining a reference file on criminal attorneys as one of your top priorities; but, based on the many unfortunate and impromptu circumstances faced by African-American families, I highly recommend this for emergency purposes. Having immediate access to an experienced criminal attorney can be just as important as having immediate access to your doctor in an unexpected or untimely fight to save your life.

Remember, the attorney client privilege law provides confidentiality protection for clients. Give your lawyer all information and in turn, ask for all information, including timeline expectations, legal needs, fee estimates, options, etc.

## Public Defender

If you don't have an attorney or access to an attorney, you have a right to request one assigned by the court. Defendants who are indigent are assigned Public Defenders. However, Public Defenders are overworked with heavy caseloads. Often, they do not have adequate funding for investigative and expert services.

In addition, ineffective or incompetent defense counsel are reasons why men and women who might otherwise have been proven innocent at trial to be sent to prison. Failure to investigate, failure to call witnesses, inability to prepare the trial (due to caseload or incompetence), are a few examples of poor lawyering; and there is always the underlying factor of potential racism or discrimination on the part of your appointed lawyer.

The following tips are recommended:

1. Because of the court-appointed lawyer's heavy caseload, he or she will never have a lot of time to discuss the case with each client. Therefore, it is important for the client to always be on time for scheduled court appearances and office meetings. If you are late, or skip a meeting for any reason, your court appointed lawyer will be less prepared to handle your case, and you will be less informed about your options.

2. A court-assigned attorney is appointed to represent his or her client, and not the client's family. Furthermore, ethical rules concerning the attorney-client privilege sometimes prevent the attorney from discussing the case with anyone other than the defendant. If family members call to find out what is going on with the case, do not be offended if the attorney does not discuss the case with them. They may attend all court proceedings to hear what is going on with the case, or they can find out by discussing the case with the defendant.

3. A family member can be helpful to the accused by bringing names, addresses and phone numbers of witnesses listed on a sheet of paper to court, or by mailing it to the attorney's office.

4. A court-assigned attorney should be interested in hearing from family members if the client has special needs requiring help. The attorney will be interested in knowing if the client has a chemical dependency, mental health issues or learning disabilities. That type of information can be used for treatment and pretrial programs.

It is at times difficult for a lawyer to determine the appropriate approach in advising a client about the merits of a guilty plea without improperly coercing a client to plea. There should be a wide range of reasonableness in deciding how a lawyer best advises a client to avoid failing, by giving appropriate advice and by not coercing the client to plead guilty. But, for the most part, courts have concluded that representation of a criminal defendant is truly "an art" and not a science; and therefore each situation is unique.

## Take Note...

You should never be rude or disrespectful to your court-appointed lawyer. If you suspect poor legal representation by your public defender, try resolving the conflict with a one-on-one meeting. Be respectful and polite. If you are still having problems, contact your attorney's supervisor. As a last resort, you may request the judge to assign you a different attorney.

Before you hire an attorney, make sure you understand the full payment process. Use this as your guideline:

### Statement of Clients Rights and Responsibilities

▼ Your attorney is providing you with this document to inform you of what you, as a client, are entitled to by law or by custom. To help prevent any misunderstanding between you and your attorney, please read this document carefully.

▼ If you ever have any questions about your rights, or about the way your case is being handled, do not hesitate to ask your attorney. He or she should be readily available to represent your best interests and keep you informed about the case.

▼ An attorney may not refuse to represent you on the basis of race, creed, color, sex, sexual orientation, age, national origin or disability.

▼ You are entitled to an attorney who will be capable of handling your case; show you courtesy and consideration at all times, represent you zealously, and preserve your confidence and secrets that are revealed in the course of the relationship.

▼ You are entitled to a written retainer agreement, which must set forth, in plain language, the nature of the relationship and the details of the fee arrangement. At your request, and before you sign the agreement, you are entitled to have your attorney clarify in writing any of its terms, or include additional provisions.

▼ You are entitled to fully understand the proposed rates and retainer fee before you sign a retainer agreement, as in any other contract.

▼ You may refuse to enter into any fee arrangement that you find unsatisfactory.

▼ Your attorney may not request a retainer fee that is non-refundable. That is, should you discharge your attorney, or should your attorney withdraw from the case, before the retainer is used up, he or she is entitled to be paid commensurate with the work performed on your case and any expenses, but must return the balance of the retainer to you. However, your attorney may enter into a minimum fee arrangement with you that provides for the payment of a specific amount below which the fee will not fall based upon the handling of the case to its conclusion.

▼ You are entitled to know the approximate number of attorneys and other legal staff members who will be working on your case at any given time and what you will be charged for the services of each.

▼ You are entitled to know in advance how you will be asked to pay legal fees and expenses, and how the retainer, if any, will be spent.

▼ At your request, and after your attorney has had a reasonable opportunity to investigate your case, you are entitled to be given an estimate of approximate future costs of your case, which estimate shall be made in good faith but may be subject to change due to facts and circumstances affecting the case.

▼ You are entitled to receive a written, itemized bill on a regular basis, at least every 60 days.

▼ You are expected to review the itemized bills sent by counsel, and to raise any objections or errors in a timely manner. Time spent in discussion or explanation of bills will not be charged to you. You are expected to be truthful in all discussions with your attorney and to provide all relevant information and documentation to enable him or her to competently prepare your case.

▼ You are entitled to be kept informed of the status of your case, and to be provided with copies of correspondence and documents prepared on your behalf or received from the court or your adversary.

▼ You have the right to be present in court at the time that conferences are held.

▼ You are entitled to make the ultimate decision on the objectives to be pursued in your case, and to make the final decision regarding the settlement of your case.

▼ Your attorney's written retainer agreement must specify under what circumstances he or she might seek to withdraw as your attorney for non-payment of legal fees. If an action or proceeding is pending, the court may give your attorney a "charging lien", which entitles your attorney to payment for services already rendered at the end of the case out of the proceeds of the final order or judgment.

▼ You are under no legal obligation to sign a confession or judgment or promissory note, or to agree to a lien or mortgage on your home to cover legal fees. Your attorney's written retainer agreement must specify whether, and under what circumstances, such security may be requested. In no event may such security interest be obtained by your attorney, without a prior court order and notice to you. An attorney's security interest in the marital residence cannot be foreclosed against you.

▼ You are entitled to have your attorney's best efforts exerted on your behalf, but no particular results can be guaranteed.

▼ If you entrust money with an attorney for an escrow deposit in your case, the attorney must safeguard the escrow in a special bank account. You are entitled to a written escrow agreement, a written receipt, and a complete record concerning the escrow. When the terms of the escrow agreement have been performed, the attorney must promptly make payment of the escrow to all persons who are entitled to it.

▼ In the event of a fee dispute you may have the right to seek arbitration. Your attorney will provide you with the necessary information regarding arbitration in the event of a fee dispute, or upon your request.

CRIME REPORT:
"MAN CLEARED IN MISCONDUCT CASE - CLAIMED POLICE BRUTALIZED HIM AND HIS HALF-BROTHER"

When my client and his girlfriend got into an argument, her sister called police for fear it might get out of hand. The argument was settled by the time the police arrived at their residence; and things got out of hand with the police instead. Without provocation, the responding police viciously beat my client and his brother with nightsticks.

The incident was provoked by the police and could have been avoided if they had acted in a professional manner upon arrival at the victims' home. After a non-jury trial, the City Judge dismissed the charges against my client, which alleged he had resisted arrest. Several members of the community picketed the courthouse to protest police brutality.

## Always Remember...

As a defendant, you should always remember that your fate rests in your lawyer's hands.

*"There are two ways of exerting one's strength; one is pushing down, the other is pulling up."*
—**Booker T. Washington**

## Chapter Two
# Know Your Rights

**I**f the police, for any reason, ever detain you, know your rights!

## Never Pick a Fight That You Can't Win

At the age of 22 years, I had my initiation into the criminal justice system when I attended the New York State Police Academy, where I would graduate as a state trooper. During that time, I had my first experience handling situations that involved resisting arrest. I had undergone six months of intense training, where I learned techniques to arrest people who did not consent to being arrested. I was taught that people who were being arrested were dangerous; they had the potential to hurt, maim, injure or kill a police officer.

When a person resists arrest the first concern is for the officer's safety; so, the matter has to be handled forcefully, quickly and effectively. If the officer takes too long to resolve the situation, he may have a crowd of people to handle rather than one, because the perpetrator can or may encourage others to join him. On the other hand, if the perpetrator is "controlled" quickly, others will be deterred from getting involved.

I learned that the perpetrator could potentially take my weapon away from me, particularly if I was involved in a wrestling match. I was taught how to use a nightstick on the knees, groin, elbows or shoulder blades, but to avoid blows to the head. I was also taught wrist throws and other takedown techniques, as well as boxing and karate.

About a year after I left the academy, a trooper at my station in Syracuse, New York was kicked in the groin by a woman and lost several weeks of work because of the injury he sustained. Apparently, he had not taken the woman seriously, due to her gender. Senior troopers constantly reminded all of the new troopers like myself, of the situation.

About seven o'clock on a summer evening, I was working alone in my patrol car when I was called to respond to a K-Mart where store security was having a problem with a shoplifter. When I arrived, I was sent to the women's accessories department; where I saw a young black female cursing out the store security manager. I was told she stole some items and wouldn't allow herself to be arrested by store security.

I tried to take control of the situation. I told the woman to turn around and place her hands behind her back, and that she was under arrest. She proceeded to curse me out. I had no choice but to take quick control of the situation because a crowd was gathering. After my repeated attempts to talk her into doing as I asked, I grabbed her wrist, pulled her arm towards me and twisted it. I then applied force to her elbow, forced her to the ground and cuffed her. The techniques that I had learned in the academy had worked.

The young woman was taken to the troop barracks and processed. I then took her to a judge who set a very high bail, because she had resisted arrest. If she had not resisted arrest and had known how to deal with a police officer, things could have turned out different. I could have simply given her an appearance ticket and she could have come to court on her own the following Tuesday night.

I felt bad for the young woman as I left her at the county jail. She was crying; she didn't have anyone to call or post her bail. I did not feel good about what had happened; but I was left with no other choice. Her actions resulted in her being forcibly arrested. It is imperative that you learn how to deal with the police and never pick a fight that you can't win.

## Dealing With Police

Police officers belong to a subculture they refer to each other as "Brothers". Suicide rates, divorce rates, and alcoholism rates are significantly higher for police officers than the rate of most occupations and the general population. Their daily routines go from extreme highs and lows. They could work for several days and face extreme boredom; then suddenly they can come across a situation and face extreme terror.

At five o'clock P.M. when most government offices are closed, the police officers are the government. They investigate fatal accidents, deliver babies, solve neighborhood disputes, recover stolen property and arrest very dangerous people. Most police officers work nights, weekends and holidays when most people are off; oftentimes, they work swing shift.

The high stress level, combined with a feeling that they are not appreciated or liked by the public, causes many police officers to become isolated and lonely. They may see the world as divided between two groups…officers and civilians.

The average black male, if confronted, by a stranger on the street who had a gun and a baseball bat would not argue with that stranger on the street. He wouldn't do anything to disrespect the stranger, for fear of getting shot or getting hit with the bat. Police officers have guns, nightsticks, chemical spray and handcuffs. He will use any of these weapons that he has at his disposal, if necessary, to effect an arrest or defend himself. The commonsense that black men use among each other that says don't mess with someone bigger and stronger than you who is armed is the same commonsense that you should apply when dealing with the police. Do not pick a fight that you cannot win.

There are some things you should do, some things you must do and some things you cannot do. Take note:

▼ Don't run! Don't touch any police officer.

▼ Keep your hands where police can see them.

▼ Don't resist, even if you believe you are innocent

▼ Remember, anything you say or do can be used against you.

▼ Be polite and respectful; never bad-mouth a police officer.

▼ Stay calm and in control of your words, body language and emotions.

▼ Don't get into an argument with the police.

▼ Don't complain on the scene or tell the police they are wrong or that you're going to file a complaint.

▼ Remember officers' badge and control car numbers.

▼ Write down everything you remember ASAP.

▼ Try to find a witness and their names and phone numbers.

▼ If you are injured, seek medical attention immediately and take photographs of the injuries as soon as possible.

▼ If you feel your rights have been violated, file a written complaint with police department's internal affairs division or civilian complaint board.

▼ Do not make any statements regarding the incident. Ask for a lawyer immediately.

## FYI...Your Right to Silence

One of the most important things you should do if you are ever detained is to exercise your right to silence. What you say to the police is always important. Anytime you feel as though you may be a suspect in a crime, once you tell a police officer you want to talk to a lawyer, he can no longer question you. If there's ever any doubt, don't ask the police officer, "Do I need to talk to a lawyer?" The officer's interest is not to encourage you to use all your constitutional protections, but rather to waive them.

## Watch Your Mouth!

Having a big mouth can and will get you arrested. Many African-American youths display a confrontational attitude, when confronted by police officers. When the officers ask youths to leave a street corner, they are often greeted with tough looks and smart talk; then, the youths in their machismo walk away in a definitely slow manner.

If you tick off a police officer off, he will find a reason to arrest you. Disturbing the peace, disorderly conduct, trespassing, blocking pedestrian traffic and loitering are discretionary charges that police officers can lay on people because they have big mouths or are disrespectful.

So, don't pick a fight you can't win. If a neighborhood thug had a gun and a stick, you wouldn't be disrespectful to him because of your own common sense. Just because a guy has a uniform on, the rules do not change.

Spending a night in jail is not fun; jails are dirty and smelly. You may find yourself sleeping on a hard bench with no pillow or blanket; and forget about supper, taking a shower or brushing your teeth. When asked to leave by a police officer, do so in a quiet and respectful manner.

# If you are ever stopped "for questioning":

▼ Be aware that it's not a crime to refuse to answer questions, but refusing to answer can make the police suspicious about you. (You can't be arrested merely for refusing to identify yourself on the street).

▼ Police may "pat-down" your clothing if they suspect a concealed weapon. Don't physically resist, but make it clear that you don't consent to any further search.

▼ Ask if you are under arrest; if you are, you must consent to being handcuffed. Do not ask any questions.

▼ Don't bad-mouth the police or run away; even if you believe what is happening to you is unreasonable. (That could lead to your arrest.)

## Reacting to a Black Man's Greatest Fear

A few years ago, I was driving my family in my newly purchased mini van on a busy suburban street. I was rear-ended twice while waiting at a green light. I got out of my car and went to the car behind me suspecting that the driver had suffered a heart attack or seizure. When I got to the car, I saw a highly intoxicated white woman behind the wheel of the car. Instinctively, I opened her car door, put the vehicle in park and took her keys.

I then felt my life was in danger; I am a two-hundred-pound black man involved in a potentially volatile situation with a drunk woman who, in her drunkenness, became belligerent and argumentative. I felt that I could have been attacked by white passers-by or attacked and arrested by the police. It was time for common sense and survival skills to take over.

After surveying the damage to my new van, I did not argue with the woman. Instead, I got back inside the van, locked the doors and called 911. I explained to the operator what had happened and remained inside my minivan. When the police officer came to the window, I rolled it down and calmly explained what had happened; I remained calm despite the fact that my young children were crying.

## Think Before You Act!

If I had not remained calm and had a dispute with the driver, I could have been met with a black man's greatest fear…a white police officer coming to the rescue in defense of the honor of a white woman; but I used common sense; I did not have to fight for my life.

### If you are stopped while driving your car:

▼ You don't have to answer a police officer's questions, but you must show your driver's license when stopped in a car. In other situations, however, you can't be arrested for refusing to identify yourself to a police officer.

▼ Upon request, you must show police your driver's license, registration and proof of insurance. In certain cases, your car can be searched without a warrant as long as the police have a probable cause. To protect yourself later, you should make it clear that you do not consent to a search. It is not lawful for police to arrest you for refusing to consent to a search.

▼ If you are given a ticket, you should sign it; otherwise you can be arrested. You can always fight the case in court later.

▼ If you're suspected of drunk driving (DWI) and refuse to take a blood, urine or breath test, your driver's license may be suspended.

▼ If police attempt to pull your car over for any reason, do not try to run away and get in a high-speed chase. If you do so, you may become involved in an accident that could seriously injure or kill you or an innocent person. When the emergency lights of a police car are on, pull over to the right side of the road as far as possible. Keep your hands visible on the steering wheel. Do not duck down or reach for anything unless instructed to do so by the police officer. Be polite to the officer and smile at him in a kind way. If you were speeding and the officer sees that you are a nice polite friendly person, he may give you a warning instead of a speeding ticket.

## If the police knock and ask to enter your home:

▼  You don't have to admit them unless they have a warrant signed by a judge.

▼  However, in some emergency situations (like a person screaming for help inside, they get an emergency phone call from your home number, or when the police are chasing someone) officers are allowed to enter and search your home without a warrant.

▼  If you are arrested, the police can search you and the area close by. If you are in a building, "close by" usually means just the room you are in.

▼  If your rights are ever violated, based on police interaction, you can discuss the matter with an attorney afterward. Always consider your safety first.

▼  You have the right to remain silent and talk to a lawyer before you talk to the police. Tell the police nothing except your name and address. Don't give any explanations, excuses or stories. You can make your defense later, in court, based on what you and your lawyer decide is best.

## If you are arrested or taken to a police station:

▼  Ask to see a lawyer immediately. If you can't pay for a lawyer, you have a right to a free one, and should ask the police how the lawyer should be contacted. Don't say anything without a lawyer.

▼ Within a reasonable time after your arrest, or booking, you have the right to make a local phone call to a lawyer, bail bondsman, relative or any other person. The police may not listen to the call to the lawyer.

▼ Sometimes you can be released without bail. If you are charged with a misdemeanor, the police officer may give you an appearance ticket allowing you to go home and appear in court on a later date. If you are polite and respectful to the arresting officer, he may release you with an appearance ticket.

▼ Do not make any decisions in your case until you have talked to a lawyer.

▼ Be careful about anything you do or say. Often times there are hidden cameras watching you even when you think you are alone.

## Victims of Police Brutality

If you are a victim of police brutality, do not contact the press or file a complaint with any agency without having first consulted the attorney who is defending you on the criminal charges. You must understand that you are a defendant in a criminal case and your first priority is to stay out of jail and avoid a criminal conviction. Statements that you make when you file a complaint against a police officer will be used against you in a criminal trial.

Furthermore, if an officer knows that you have filed a complaint against him or knows that you are going to sue him, he will use whatever influence he has with the prosecutor to insure that you are vigorously prosecuted. If you are convicted of criminal charges, a civil lawsuit, in most cases, will have little or no value. If a jury knows that you plan on filing a lawsuit, they can consider that as an issue in assessing your credibility. If the charges against you are dismissed, then you should consider filing a lawsuit.

## CRIME REPORT:
## "COCAINE COUNTS DISMISSED AGAINST THREE
## WHO CLAIMED RETALIATORY ARRESTS BY POLICE"

A judge dismissed cocaine trafficking charges against three people who claimed they were marked for retaliation by an elite Buffalo police unit because they had been acquitted in an earlier case. As attorney for the three defendants, I argued that arrests were "clearly retaliatory"; I had obtained statements from witnesses who confirmed that the defendants were targets of ethnic slurs and racial harassment, when they were booked at Buffalo Police headquarters. The prosecutors admitted in court that they had problems proving the new charges and they reduced the level of the charges from felonies to misdemeanors after tests revealed that nine packets of suspected cocaine found in a van turned out to contain less than an eighth of an ounce of cocaine. Fortunately, the defendants did not resist arrest; so there was no ground for adding other charges that could impose a harsher sentence.

## Always Remember...

After consulting your attorney and with his advice, you may file a complaint against an officer for police brutality at:

1. The local chapter of the American Civil Liberties Union.
2. The local chapter of the NAACP.
3. The Internal Affairs Bureau of the Police Department.
4. The Police Civilian Review Board.
5. The Office of your Municipal Government Representative.
6. The FBI

*"It is certain, in any case, that ignorance, allied with power, is
the most ferocious enemy justice can have."*
**—James Baldwin**

## Chapter Three
# Caught Up In the
# Criminal Justice System

Y ou've been accused of a crime and are being processed through
the Criminal Justice System. And now, you are suddenly one person
against thousands. According to the Criminal Justice System, all
crimes are considered to be "public wrongs" committed against the
community, not just private wrongs committed against the victim(s).

Federal laws and procedures apply to cases prosecuted in the federal
court system; most crimes, however, are prosecuted in the state court
system, which is where my jurisdiction lies. Although I practice law
in the State of New York, I have attempted to write this book using
general guidelines that are commonplace throughout the nation.
Keep in mind, however, within constitutional limits, each state is
allowed to write its own classification and definition of a crime; and
able to adopt its own procedural rules and criminal laws.

The criminal justice system is actually made up of a group of agencies
responsible for particular stages of a criminal matter or case. The
Police Officer makes the arrest and files the report, the Police Detective investigates the crime; the Prosecutor determines the charges

made against the accused and tries the case; the judge oversees the court procedures; and the Corrections Personnel manage the incarceration process of the defendant. Although to the defendant, they are seemingly one unit, each agency is under its own jurisdiction and may or may not have a cohesive relationship.

The judge may sentence a person to probation. When a person is released from jail, he or she is placed under the supervision of a Parole Officer.

## Your Identity Can Lead To Your Conviction

If you are arrested for a criminal offence, there's a strong possibility that you will end up in a line-up. There are three types of identification procedures: a show-up, a line-up, and a photographic array.

▼ A Show-up is a police arranged confrontation that occurs near the crime scene. The suspect is detained by police and is shown to the crime victim or witness who is the asked to identify him or her. There is a danger of misidentification when this procedure is used because when people see someone in police custody they assume that the police got the right person.

▼ A Line-up occurs at the police station. The defendant and five or more people of similar stature and dress stand on a stage holding numbered cards. The witness is situated behind a one way mirror and is asked to identify the person who committed the crime by number.

▼ A Photographic Array is a series of six or more numbered photographs of similar people that are put on display for a witness. The witness is asked to pick out the photograph of the person who committed the crime.

The fairness of the identification procedure can be challenged at a pre-trial hearing. If a judge determines that the procedure used was unfair and unconstitutionally suggestive he or she will issue a ruling prohibiting testimony or evidence about the identification in court. In some cases, the suppression of identification testimony results in the dismissal of the charges.

As a participant of an "in-person" lineup, you'll be grouped with other individuals of similar stature and similarly attired. The group will then be given a number and lined-up in a room with a one-way mirror that enables the crime victim to see the individuals, but not be seen by them.

You don't have to be present to be part of a photo line-up; but if a crime victim identifies you from a photo or mug shot, you can justifiably be picked up by the police for questioning or arrested and charged with a crime.

If you commit a crime and you are still at the scene when the police arrive, the victim can make an identity right on the spot and instigate your immediate arrest.

## Always Remember...

With the high availability of video cameras in so many retail establishments, parking lots and other public places, you can leave a video imprint just about anywhere, at anytime, making your positive identity almost certain. *Just say no!*

## "Smile...You're On Candid Camera!"

A few years ago, I represented two female college freshmen during the Christmas Holiday season. Both girls came from upper-middle-class backgrounds in the New York City Metropolitan area. They went to a suburban mall to buy and steal Christmas presents. One of the girls blocked the view of the store clerk while the other placed merchandise into a shopping bag. Store security responded and tried to take the girls into custody; they resisted and were taken in by force.

When both girls' parents hired me, they explained to me that their daughters were wrongfully arrested and charged with taking items they had not paid for; and that they were both good kids who wouldn't lie. I was told to check the girls' receipts and they would match the supposedly stolen items. Because the girls had spent the night in jail, the parents were eager to commence with a false arrest/ malicious prosecution lawsuit.

I attended the court proceeding and made arrangements to meet with store security immediately after leaving court.

The security manager took me to the viewing room where there was a large panel of forty television monitors, on which there was live close-up footage of shoppers throughout the store. The security manager then played a video tape of my clients as they entered the store; it showed them stealing and resisting arrest, which was an ugly scene. The parents were shocked when I called them with the details.

Fortunately, I was able to get the criminal charges dismissed after the girls completed court ordered community service. Both girls went on to graduate college. Parents must get involved with their children's lives; advise them that when they steal, they will eventually get caught. Unfortunately, it doesn't always end up as well.

## Misidentification, False Confessions, and the Wrongful Conviction of the Innocent

In 2000 Gary Graham was executed in Huntsville, Texas for a murder that he did not commit. A jury convicted him of shooting Bobby Lambert to death in a robbery outside a supermarket in 1991. The evidence against Graham was largely the testimony of a single witness who picked Graham out of a lineup. The jury that convicted Graham never heard from two witnesses who claimed that Graham was not the man who committed the murder. Three jurors stated that they would not have convicted Graham had they heard the testimony of the two eyewitnesses who claimed Graham was not the murderer.

The Reverend Jesse Jackson urged Bush to stop the execution; but the then Texas Governor George Bush refused to pardon Graham and allowed him to be murdered by lethal injection. Reverend Jackson prayed with Graham the night before the execution.

In 1985 Steven Avens was arrested for rape and attempted murder in Manitonic County, Wisconsin. The victim testified that she was sure Avery was the man who raped her. Avery was sentenced to thirty-two years in prison. After serving seventeen years in prison, he was freed when DNA evidence cleared him.

## Take Note!

The "Innocence Project", founded by famed OJ Simpson attorney Barry Scheck, lists one hundred twenty-five people whose convictions were overturned by DNA evidence. Many of the convictions that were overturned were cases of mistaken identity; other wrongful convictions were obtained with false confessions.

As a defense attorney, I am always concerned about the danger of misidentification, whenever I have a client who is ordered to appear in a lineup. There is always the possibility that the police hint or suggest to the victim who the suspect is and, thereby, influence the identification procedure. There is also the danger of possible misidentification when the lineup standing is significantly different in appearance from my client.

Early in my career as a defense attorney, I represented two African-American upper middle class suburban youths who were accused of a BB gun robbery of another youth. The judge in the case ordered my clients to appear in a lineup. Both of my clients were light-skinned and had a suburban, preppy look about them.

I knew, from my experience as a prosecutor, that the police officers get line-up stand-ins from prisons and detention facilities. Sometimes police go to homeless shelters and find stand-ins who are willing to appear in a lineup for ten dollars.

I had my client's parents contact their friends and borrow their sons who looked similar to my clients in skin color, hairstyle and size, to accompany me to the lineup. I convinced the detective to allow the people that I brought to the lineup to serve as stand-ins. Neither of my clients was picked out of the lineup, and charges against both defendants were dropped.

While I was writing this book, an attorney brought to my attention a pending case, where his client was misidentified in a shooting incident. The attorney told me that there had been a disturbance outside a bar that had a predominantly white clientele. His client, who was a young African-American man, ran from the scene and was accused of firing shots. Minutes after the shooting, police arrested his client; nine eyewitnesses, who were white, positively identified the young African-American man.

One week after the shooting, it was discovered that the shooting incident was caught on videotape by a surveillance camera at a nearby hotel. At the attorney's urging, prosecutors obtained the tape one day before it was scheduled to be rewound and re-used by hotel security. The tape proved that the young African-American man did not do the shooting. He was released from custody and prosecutors are considering a dismissal of the charges. This case illustrates the dangers and unreliability of cross-racial identification.

One of the things that can be done to reduce the charges of innocent people being misidentified and accused of crimes is to make blind line-ups a requirement in criminal cases.

A blind lineup is a procedure, where the witness to the crime views two lineups; the suspect appears in just one lineup. The detective who is conducting the lineup is unaware of who the suspect is; and the witness is unaware of which lineup the suspect is in. The blind lineup procedure makes it impossible for the detective conducting the lineup to tip off the witness with body language or verbal hints as to who the suspect is. Although blind lineups are not perfect, if they are implemented, the dangers of a wrongful conviction are reduced.

Sometimes a witness to a crime is shown photograph arrays in order to identify someone who is suspected of committing a crime. A photo array generally is a display of six numbered photographs of different people with similar features. It is shown to a witness who is then asked to identify the perpetrator of the crime.

Photo arrays are shown to witnesses in situations where there is no judicial oversight or defense input. Hypothetically, a detective can go to the home of a witness with a photo array and cheat by suggesting to the witness who the suspect is. Because there is no independent witness to the "cheating" the tainted procedure is never discovered or challenged.

It should be a legal requirement that all photo array identification procedures are videotaped. Video cameras are readily available to the law enforcement agencies and they capture the truth. A legal requirement for photographic array identification procedures to be video-taped will serve to protect the innocent.

I also urge a legal requirement that all statements or confessions of the accused are videotaped or audio-taped in order to be admissible in court. This requirement will ensure that what police allege that the defendant said is accurate. Videotaping or audiotaping will also ensure that the witness wasn't tricked, coerced or threatened to give the police a statement against his or her interest.

## Alibi Defenses

Many people in the general public think that an Alibi Defense is a good defense. It is often used in cases involving mistaken identification. If a defense is "I was at home with my mother or girlfriend at the time when the crime was committed" you are in for a tough battle. Prosecutors with arguments that the family member doesn't want to see a loved one convicted of a crime and is simply lying often persuade jurors.

We live in an era of high technology. In order for an alibi defense to be effective, Jurors are persuaded by independent technical evidence establishing a person's whereabouts at a certain place and time. Supermarkets and stores often have stamped security cameras. Cashiers at stores and supermarkets give receipts with dates and times. ATM's give time stamped receipts and photograph the transactions. Cell phone and telephone records, movie theater receipts, video rental receipts, service station video surveillance also can be useful aids in an alibi defense.

## Think Before You Act!

If you want to raise an alibi defense, you must brainstorm and give your attorney ideas where he can subpoena evidence of your whereabouts. You must give him receipts, credit card records, cell phone records and other information that will be helpful in establishing your defense.

A recent client who I secured an acquittal for, by use of an alibi defense, was "Mark". Mark was walking home wearing a bright red shirt and black pants. A woman was robbed on the previous day by a man she described as "a black man with a bright red shirt and black pants". The day after she was robbed, she saw Mark and mistakenly thought he was the man who robbed her. She followed him to the house and called the police on her cell phone. The police arrived and asked Mark to come outside. The woman identified him as the robber.

I took Mark's case to trial. If convicted, he faced a possible sentence of 12 ½ to 25 years imprisonment. Mark was at City Hall paying a parking ticket when the crime occurred. His mother drove him to the Parking Violations Bureau. She couldn't find a parking space, so she kept circling the building. At 11:15A.M. Mark's mother called him from her cell phone to find out what was taking so long.

At the trial the woman pointed out Mark as the robber; she claimed that there was no doubt in her mind. Needless to say, with his mother's testimony and with a paper trail of evidence, including cell phone records and parking fine payment receipts that supported his alibi, I was able to get an acquittal for Mark.

Organization in your life and a good attorney may one day save your life.

## Crime Classifications

There are several classifications of crimes, which may vary from state to state. A Petty Offense or Infraction is a less serious crime, such as: Disturbing the Peace, Loitering or a Traffic Violation. A Misdemeanor, which may carry up to one year in prison, often includes: Assault, Battery, Indecent Exposure, Simple Theft, Telephone Harassment and Trespassing. A Felony is the most serious crime, which can carry up to life in prison or even the death penalty; those charges would include: Aggravated Stalking, Arson, Carjacking, Drugs, Grand Theft, Forgery, Burglary, Arson, Manslaughter, Murder, Rape/Sexual Assault. You cannot be charged with any crime, however, unless one or more element relating to that crime is present.

In the Criminal Justice System, you are entitled to the protection of the United States Constitution and its applicable laws.

As the Defendant in a criminal case, you are presumed innocent and have no Burden of Proof; the state has the entire burden of proving "beyond a reasonable doubt" that you committed a crime.

## Will Justice Prevail?

The County or State Prosecutor a.k.a. District Attorney decides whether or not to pursue a state charge. The U.S. Attorney's office decides whether or not to charge for Federal cases. After police have completed their investigation, the file and all reports are provided to the prosecutor's office for consideration. For misdemeanors, police may either recommend that charges be filed or file the charges themselves. Alternately, a crime victim may also pursue a misdemeanor charge against a defendant.

Prosecutors also have the discretion of deciding what to charge; for example, a less serious misdemeanor, rather than a felony could be charged in a given situation. The prosecutor may also choose not to file a charge at all, usually based on one or more of the following reasons:

▼ Convinced of a suspect's innocence

▼ More than reasonable doubt of the suspect's guilt

▼ Reluctance of a key witness to testify

▼ Cooperation of the accused in the arrest of others

▼ A legal element of the case is not present

▼ Circumstances of the crime are such that a jury is unlikely to convict

▼ Illegal conduct of the police in obtaining evidence.

## Your Arraignment

Shortly after the arrest, the accused (defendant) has an Initial Appearance or "Arraignment" before a judge. At this time, the defendant is informed of the charges and provides an opportunity for the defendant to enter a plea of not guilty, guilty, or no contest. If the plea is not guilty, the case will continue towards a trial; with a guilty plea, the defendant admits to the charges and receives a conviction; when a "no contest" plea is entered, the defendant does not admit to the crime, but agrees to accept a conviction from the court.

At the first hearing, an attorney will be appointed for the defendant if he or she cannot afford private counsel. The defendant has a right to have the charges read, but many defendants waive this right. The judge will make the decision at this time to grant or deny bail and will schedule the next appearance at this time.

## Always Remember...

With a no contest plea, because the facts of the case are not proven, they cannot be used in a later civil trial as evidence of guilt. (It will be presumed that the plea is not guilty). "No contest" is not an option in New York State and many other states.

The three common methods by which a crime can be charged with are: complaint, information and indictment. A Complaint is an accusatory instrument signed by a police officer who does not witness the crime. If the complaint charges a petty offense of misdemeanor in order for the charges to be legally sufficient, the judge will order the prosecutor to obtain a sworn written statement from the person who has direct knowledge of the crime. After the prosecutor complies with the judge's request, then the complaint has been legally converted to an Information.

For felony cases, defendants are charged in the lower courts with an accusatory instrument known as a felony complaint. When the prosecutor presents evidence to a Grand Jury that is sufficient, then the Grand Jury issues an accusatory instrument known as an Indictment and the case is then transferred to a higher superior court.

## The Preliminary Hearing and Grand Jury Process

The judge, who presides over a criminal case, has a duty to remain impartial. Whenever a legal question comes up, he or she makes decisions based on the laws, procedures and previous case decisions. It's up to the defendant to decide whether to proceed with a preliminary hearing or to waive the case to the Grand Jury. If the Grand Jury indicts the case, the charges are transferred to a higher court. The judge approves continuances; makes the final decision on whether the state has enough evidence to proceed and what evidence can be presented; and rules on any objections that may occur during the trial. If no jury is requested, the judge will preside over a "bench trial".

The Preliminary Hearing is usually held soon after the defendant's initial court appearance. The purpose of this hearing is to determine whether probable cause exists that a crime was committed, and that this defendant committed the crime. This hearing will be held before the judge. The police officer will testify and the victim may also be called as a witness. The defendant does not have to produce any witnesses, but does have the right to cross-examine any prosecution witness at this hearing. After the witnesses have been presented, the judge will either determine that there is sufficient evidence to continue to trial or can dismiss the case and release the defendant.

The Grand Jury is comprised of twenty-three Grand Jurors. Sixteen Grand Jurors are required to hear evidence; twelve Grand Jurors are needed to vote an indictment. The prosecutor plays the role as the Grand Jurors' legal advisor and presents evidence to the Grand Jury.

## FYI...The Grand Jury Process

The grand jury process, which may be used either in addition to, or instead of a preliminary hearing, determines whether there is probable cause to charge the defendant. Like any other jury, the grand jury is made up of citizens selected from either the voter or motor vehicle registration lists.

More often than not, the grand jury will render a "True Bill", upon which a warrant is issued and the defendant is arrested; this is more probable than not because only the prosecutor presents evidence at the grand jury hearing. If no bill is issued, however, the case does not proceed.

If you have been charged with a crime, you may either be entitled to an appointed attorney or, providing that you have the financial resources, hiring one. Your attorney's goal is to assure that your rights are not violated and ultimately to obtain a dismissal or acquittal, whenever possible, or obtain the best possible plea bargain. The best way to obtain either will be to utilize any of the following strategies:

▼ Entrapment or Involuntary Act

▼ Insufficient Evidence

▼ Mistaken Identity

▼ Self Defense

▼ Unfit or Insane Defendant

▼ Rights of the defendant have been violated by the state while they gathered evidence.

▼ Duress—the defendant was forced or threatened to commit the crime

▼ Lack of proof beyond a reasonable doubt

## Pre-Trial Motions

Typically, criminal court cases have lengthy delays because the state and the defendant need time to gather evidence and investigate the case. The legal process for obtaining the necessary time is called a "Motion", which is an oral or written request made to a judge who may either grant or decline the request. Here are six types of motions, which may be filed in a criminal case:

1.  Motion to Dismiss—Can be filed by the Defendant if the charge fails to meet legal requirements or if the state failed to meet his or her rights to a speedy trial. Can be filed by the State if they decide to proceed on some of the charges and drop the others.

2.  Motion to Suppress Identification—Can be filed by the Defendant to preclude the admission into evidence at trial by a police arranged identification procedure that is unconstitutionally impermissible. For example, a tall thin dark skinned Black male suspect is placed in a line-up with five short fat light skinned Black males – then such line-up is simply unfair.

3. Motion to Suppress Statements—Can be filed by the Defendant to stop the State from using admissions, confessions or other statements that were taken by force or without the Defendant being properly advised of his or her right to remain silent or right to counsel.

4. Motion for Suppress Physical Evidence—Can be filed by the Defendant to challenge the legality of the search and seizure of evidence by police. If a judge rules that the search was conducted without probable cause or without the consent of the Defendant, then the evidence seized cannot be used at trial.

5. Motion for Change of Judge or Venue—Can be used by the Defendant if, for instance, the judge is determined to be prejudiced or if there is negative pretrial publicity that would keep the Defendant from receiving a fair trial in the particular jurisdiction.

6. Motions for Discovery—At the Defendant's request, the prosecution must provide police reports, criminal records of prosecution witnesses, statements of prosecutor's witnesses, scientific reports, photographs, diagrams, maps, drawings, tape recordings and other potential exhibits.

## Advice While Your Case Is Pending

▼ If you move or change your telephone number, let your attorney know immediately. Sometimes you may be required to attend court on short notice. If you fail to appear in court, the judge may issue a warrant for your arrest.

▼ Keep a calendar or diary to remind you when you must appear in court. Do not expect to receive a notice of a court date in the mail. Sometimes the only notice that you will get will be from the judge in court when he or she says what date your case is adjourned to.

▼ Do not write a statement of facts on paper without talking to your attorney. In many jurisdictions, the defense attorney must turn over the prosecutor's statements made by defense witnesses. You will be disadvantaged if the prosecutor has your statement in advance.

▼ If you write or receive any letters or other correspondence pertaining to your case, keep copies of each and every document and forward the document to your attorney. (Once you have retained an attorney, however, he or she will maintain a file of your records and maintain communications with police, witnesses, prosecutors and others involved in the case).

## CRIME REPORT:
## "MOTHER INDICTED IN DEATH OF BABY:
## DEFENDANT CALLED RETARDED"

My client, a mentally retarded woman was indicted in the death of her 9-month old daughter who died after she gave the baby anti- depressant pills because she wanted her to stop crying and go to sleep.

With the assistance of a kind African-American female doctor who was familiar with my client's medical condition. We were able to convince the District Attorney that the woman did not intend to kill her baby. She was allowed to plea to the reduced charge of criminally negligent homicide and was sentenced to probation. The doctor and I provided the woman professional services free of charge.

At sentencing I told the court that my client was mentally retarded and would not have the mental capacity to understand the effects of the pills; and that they had come from a container without a safety cap.

## Always Remember...

If you are accused of a crime, you immediately become a party to the case. Whether you were the actual "hands-on" perpetrator, an accomplice, or just along for the ride, you can be arrested as a willing participant.

*"God gives each of us our own unique gifts.*
*It is our job to recognize these gifts, nurture them and*
*utilize them to live up to our full potential."*
—Bishop T. D. Jakes

## Chapter Four

# Your Appearance and Conduct In Court:

## Don't Let A Negative First Impression Work Against You

How a defendant and his family act and dress in the Courthouse could have an impact on the outcome of the case. Prosecutors, Judges and Jurors are very observant, and make mental notes about everything they see about the Defendant and his family's behavior and dress. Bailiffs, court clerks, secretaries and court reporters talk with prosecutors and judges about rude behavior, foul language, and arguing that they see outside the courtroom.

Before entering the courtroom, remove your coat and hat. The next rule that anyone entering a courtroom should observe is to be quiet. Sit quietly and wait until your case is called. If you need to ask a Bailiff or clerk a question, do so in a polite and respectful manner.

Small children should be left at home. Sometimes people mistakenly believe that if they take small children to court that are related to the accused, that a judge will have sympathy and release the accused from custody. In most instances, when small children are brought to court, they are noisy and annoy the Judge and courtroom personnel. Eventually, the entire family that brought the children is asked to leave.

Your dress in the courtroom should be conservative. I suggest that, while on trial, my male clients wear dark suits and ties; if they are uncomfortable in a suit, I always insist on a dress shirt or polo shirt with a collar (never wear a tee-shirt) and dress or khaki slacks (not jeans). I had a client that followed my instructions, and on the first day of trial wore a suit. The problem was that the suit he wore was a bright purple. He looked like a pimp, not only to me, but to everyone else in the courtroom, as well.

Men should have conservative haircuts; braids are inappropriate. Females should wear business attire, preferably classic suits; if you prefer to wear a dress or skirt, make sure that it is not too tight or too short and worn with a top that has some type of collar. Women can wear braids, as long as they are not overbearing; they should be neat and unadorned; but, of course, classic hairstyles are always best.

When a Defendant and his or her family appears in the courtroom, there may also be people in the courtroom present who are witnesses against the Defendant. Family members and Defendants should avoid intimidating glares and snide remarks towards witnesses and their families. Such conduct will lead to expulsion from the courtroom and may lead to an arrest.

When addressing the court, a Defendant must speak clearly, using proper Standard English; "Ebonics" and street talk are okay for the hood, but never in the courtroom. I have won acquittals for clients simply because I prepared my client and witnesses to use standard English, while the prosecutor's witnesses spoke in "Ebonics".

Anytime the Judge enters or leaves the courtroom, everyone must stand until directed to sit. Failure to stand at the appropriate time can lead to an expulsion from the courtroom. Failure to stand also leaves a poor impression that may have a negative impact on the resulting disposition of the case.

## Take Note!

▼ Cell phones and pagers must be turned off during court proceedings. I have witnessed cell phones and pages being confiscated, and then the offending party being thrown out of the courtroom for violating this rule.

▼ Chewing gum is forbidden in courtrooms. Nothing is more embarrassing than having a bailiff yell at you because you are chewing gum.

▼ Sleeping is certainly forbidden. If you are watching courtroom proceedings and cannot stay awake, step out into the hallway.

## Let's Recap! Your Appearance Advisory

▼ You must always come to court dressed in a neat, clean and conservative way. Do not wear T-shirts, sweatshirts, baggy jeans, sneakers or flashy jewelry. (Females should not wear tight and revealing clothes.)

▼ Men should always wear a shirt with a collar, dress pants, leather shoes and a jacket and tie, if possible. Braids are not appropriate; a short, neat haircut is recommended.

▼ When seated in the audience waiting for your case to be called, sit up straight in the chair; don't slouch; sit still and don't fidget.

▼ Don't talk while you are waiting in the courtroom. If you must say something to your lawyer, it would be better to step out of the courtroom. However, when and if courtroom conversation is necessary, keep your voice down. Loud talking will draw negative attention to yourself and may cause a courtroom deputy to remove you.

▼ When standing in the courtroom, adjust your posture; stand straight and tall. When walking, take easy strides; don't bounce or bop.

▼ Show respect to the judge; respond to him or her as "Your Honor."

▼ Never be late for a court appearance.

▼ Bring family members to court with you. Prosecutors and judges often give breaks to offenders when they are convinced that there is family support.

CRIME REPORT:
"BEING BLACK IN AMERICA —
ONE MAN'S IMAGE IS ANOTHER MAN'S PERIL"

In the trial of OJ Simpson, the factors that played to his advantage generally work to the disadvantage of the vast majority of African-American defendants. Simpson had virtually unlimited resources, a predominantly black jury that identified with him along racial grounds, and celebrity status. Most African-American defendants, by contrast, can- not afford an attorney, much less a "dream team"; and their fate is usually decided by predominantly or exclusively white juries. And most African-American defendants find that their image is linked in America's mind not with celebrity, but with criminality. (Source: The Champion – "No Equal Justice – How the Criminal Justice System Uses Inequality")

## Always Remember...

Remember, your actions are always being watched. Try to make a good impression. Judges and prosecutors often give breaks to offenders who are neatly dressed and display some manners.

"When I discover who I am, I'll be free."
—Ralph Ellison

## Chapter Five
# The 411 About Bail

Defendants are usually eligible for release while they await their trial. In order to gain that release, they are sometimes required to give only their word and signature; this is referred to as "Personal Recognizance". Most often, however, defendants are required to pay money or provide another type of security, which insures their intent to return to court. This would include signing a bond, which states what was posted for bail (money, house, etc.). The amount of bail may be preset in some crimes; but, usually with serious felonies, a bail hearing will be held to determine the conditions and cost of the bail, depending on the circumstances of the case, such as:

▼ The strength of the prosecutor's case.

▼ Potential danger of the Defendant to the community

▼ Were there any injuries made to victims?

▼ Does the defendant have a prior criminal history?

▼ Will there be a threat to the victim(s) if the defendant is released?

▼ The community ties of the Defendant.

▼ The seriousness of the charges.

▼ Have bench warrants been issued in the past?

▼ Is the Defendant employed?

Some jurisdictions allow a defendant to post a percentage of the court-ordered bail amount; the court is entitled to an administration fee and will return the balance of the deposit as long as the defendant makes all court appearances and meets the conditions of the bond; a failure to appear, results in a forfeiture of the deposit. If the defendant cannot deposit the required amount, or if the court denies bail, the defendant will remain in jail while awaiting trial.

## Always Remember...

I must precaution you, that once you enter the criminal justice system, you are at risk of being discriminated against. As I stated in a previous chapter, racism and discrimination occur at many levels of the criminal justice system, including bail hearings. For example, I recently noted and compared two circumstances that occurred while I was in court with my client. One situation involved a black defendant who I represented on a drug offense; his bail was set at $50,000. Another situation involved a white defendant, also appearing in court that day, held for the homicide of his wife; his bail was also set at $50,000. In this instance, the scales of justice were certainly unbalanced.

## Making Bail:

Next to hiring a competent criminal defense attorney, the most important function that a family can provide for an accused is helping the accused make bail. Most defendants who make bail do not return to jail for the charges they are accused of for the following reasons.

▼ A Defendant who makes bail can provide valuable assistance to his attorney. He can locate witnesses and bring them to his attorney's office. He can go to the crime scene with his attorney, or phone a private investigator and explain events that occurred so that the attorney can take photographs and have a better understanding of what occurred.

▼ A Defendant who makes bail can come to court looking "less guilty". He is treated better and looked upon more favorably by prosecutors, judges and jurors when he is clean-shaven, properly groomed and dressed appropriately.

A Defendant who makes bail can take rehabilitative steps that will make him a better candidate for a favorable plea bargain and sentence. Examples are:

▼ Getting a job – I have often convinced judges to sentence clients to probation who are working. Employed defendants contribute to society by paying taxes. They are less likely to be re-arrested while employed.

▼ Getting treatment – Defendants who have addictions to drugs, alcohol, or gambling can seek treatment on their own, or with court assistance. If prosecutors and judges are convinced that a Defendant is addressing areas that are the root of the problem, they will be more inclined toward leniency. Some Defendants need psychological counseling or anger management counseling.

▼ Continued education – Unfortunately, the vast majority of prisoners lack a high school diploma. I always advise my clients who haven't graduated from high school to get a general equivalency diploma, and those who have graduated high school pursue a college degree, or attend trade school.

If you are out on bail pending trial, there are specific mandatory conditions, which must be maintained. Your attorney should make sure that you have a copy of the court order listing the conditions of your pre-trial release; you must make sure that you:

▼ Appear at all court dates
▼ Commit no crimes

▼  Do not leave the state

▼  Follow all stipulations and court orders

When should family members not post bail for a loved one?

There are exceptions to the rule that is best for the accused to be free on bail while awaiting trial disposition, or trial of a criminal case. If the Defendant is likely to commit future crimes while out on bail, it is not recommended that the family assist with bail. If the client is addicted to narcotics, or is out of control, do not assist him or her with bail because they will simply make more problems for themselves.

I once represented a client I'll call "Benny". He was in his early 20's and addicted to crack cocaine. Benny had a four-year-old son. Both Benny and his son lived with Benny's father. Benny sold drugs and robbed people to support his habit. His father hired me to represent him on a few minor charges, all of which were dismissed on technicalities, or plea-bargained to a time-served disposition. I asked Benny when he was going to stop smoking dope and he proudly told me "never".

Benny was arrested on a robbery. I asked his father not to bail him out, because I knew he was out of control, and would cause himself more trouble. A week after Benny got out of jail, he tried to rob a drug dealer. In the robbery attempt, the dealer shot and killed Benny. He would probably be alive today, had he not gotten out on bail.

I recently represented a 19-year-old man named "Tony" who lived with his parents in a middle-class suburban home. Federal Agents arrested him for being involved with a small ring of people who brought drugs from Canada into the United States.

Tony's parents had been having problems with his behavior for the past year. He would violate curfews, use profanity with his parents, and come home drunk.

Tony's parents bailed him out. Two weeks later he was driving while intoxicated. He got involved in a high-speed chase with police and wrecked the car. Fortunately, he was not killed. However, he faced additional charges in state court for resisting arrest, driving intoxicated, reckless driving and other charges.

## FYI...Forms of Bail

▼ **Cash:** The responsible party puts up cash.

▼ **Property:** The responsible party allows a lien to be placed upon their real property.

▼ **Bond:** Obtained by purchasing a bail bond from an insurance company.

▼ **Signature:** The responsible party agrees that a civil judgment will be entered against them if the Defendant does not appear in court.

▼ **Partially-secured:** The responsible party gives the court 10% of the bail amount and agrees to a civil judgment of the remainder if the accused fails to appear.

Bail has a big impact on the direction your life can take. It could be a determining factor in living your life as a career criminal or could even have an impact that's as serious as "life or death".

Discuss your bail with your attorney, understand its benefits; and if you are financially able to post it, use it to "Save Your Life".

CRIME REPORT:
"ARE THE SCALES OF JUSTICE
UNBALANCED BY RACISM?"

I recently represented a couple that was arrested on charges of disorderly conduct and resisting arrest. While they were being arraigned, they were also charged with writing bad checks (the 2-year old check charges had stemmed from the theft of the couple's checkbook). This is a prime example of being caught up in the system by petty offenses that could ultimately destroy your life. The incident began when the co-defendant, an African-American, lost a student government election, which he claimed was illegal; a Black Student Union was formed shortly thereafter. Fortunately, they were released on their own recognizance. Eventually, they made restitution and their cases were resolved without them getting criminal records.

## Always Remember...

If you do not make bail, you should take advantage of every program available in the institution you are in while awaiting trial. All institutions have religious services. Many have GED programs, alcohol and drug rehabilitation programs. Any self-improvement activities will not only serve towards the goal of obtaining a better resolution of the case; but it will also serve to make you a better person.

*"Freedom is the right to choose: the right to create
for oneself the alternatives of choice. Without the
possibility of choice and the exercise of choice a man
is not a man but a member, an instrument, a thing."*
—Archibald Macleish

Chapter Six
# Understanding the Role of a Jury: Your Life Is In Their Hands

If you walk into the courtroom and you're told your client is not going to be executed, in the world of capital defenders, you've won.

Jonathan Parker's death penalty jury trial was the first ever in Erie County and only the third in the state of New York since the state's death penalty had began in 1995. The purpose of the penalty phase was to give the jury a more complete picture of the defendant. It was up to my defense team to convince the jurors to vote against Parker's execution; we had an opportunity to call on his family and friends, psychologists and others to show the jurors a more complete portrait of my client than was shown during the murder trial.

Only jurors at least open to considering the death penalty can serve in such cases. In a trial of an African-American suspect for the death of an African-American policeman, that consideration played a major part in selecting a jury which included only one African-American member, as an alternate. An all white jury was selected; and I wondered if they would be able to see past their pre-conceived biases and stereotypes of all young "inner city" black men as "thugs" or drug dealers in order to give my client a fair trial.

Under the death penalty statute, jurors decide on several possible mitigating factors as they determine the defendant's fate and they choose from two options: voting for the death penalty; or voting for life in prison without parole, if they cannot decide unanimously. If they do nothing, the judge makes the final decision.

By a twist of fate, the jury voted against the death penalty.

## A Jury of One's Peers

Can blacks receive a fair trial in front of an all-white jury? What can be done to assure that more blacks serve on juries? How does our system operate? What are the roles and responsibilities of jurors? This chapter will answer these questions and equip you with survival techniques during the fight for your life.

The Rodney King and OJ Simpson cases demonstrate how America is divided among racial lines about the fairness of our jury system.

When the officers captured on videotape beating Rodney King were acquitted in the first jury trial, African-Americans and Hispanics rioted because of pent-up frustrations about perceived unfairness in the Judicial System (58 innocent people died during the riots).

Whites mourned the acquittal of OJ Simpson while African-Americans applauded, and his defense attorney Johnnie Cochran became a national hero. (For many, the verdict was a sign of hope. Historically, the murder of two whites, implicating an African-American, would have been just cause for a lynching; but because recent laws, allowing a predominantly African-American jury, OJ was granted a jury of his peers.

## The Origin of a Jury Trial

Our jury system can be traced back to England. In the year 1215 King John I signed the Magna Carta, and the concept of a jury of one's peers was first guaranteed. The Magna Carta proclaimed "No free man shall be taken or imprisoned or outlawed or exiled or in any way destroyed...except by the lawful judgment of his peers and the law of the land." The early English juries were composed of nobles who forced the king to sign the Magna Carta.

The American Colonies adopted the English jury system. References to a trial by jury of one's peers can be found in the discussions of the first Continental Congress of 1774, and in the Declaration of Independence. After the Revolutionary War, the United States Constitution was adopted. Article III of the Constitution provides that "the trial of all crimes, except in cases of impeachment, shall be by jury, and such trials shall be held in the state where the said crimes shall have been committed." Finally, the Sixth Amendment of the Constitution was passed, and guaranteed the right of a jury trial in state courts. It provides that a person accused of a crime has the right to a trial"...by an impartial jury of the state and district wherein the crime shall have been committed."

Blacks were not allowed to have jury trials, or allowed to serve on juries until after the civil war, because they were considered property, and not people. In 1850 the United States heard the case of a "colored man" named Strauder, from West Virginia; he sought to have his murder trial removed from West Virginia State Court to Federal Court because West Virginia law excluded "coloreds" from juries. The Supreme Court in the landmark case of *Strauder vs. West Virginia* found the West Virginia law unconstitutional.

## The Jury Selection Process

When a case is scheduled for trial, the Judge or a Court Administrator will notify the Jury Commissioner, who will randomly select a group of potential jurors from the computer. Jury summonses are then mailed out to the potential jurors directing them to appear for jury selection. Generally, between 50 and 100 people are requested, depending on the complexity of the case.

## FYI...Jury Selection

The process of selecting a jury begins when the Jury Commissioner composes a list of potential jurors. This list is derived from a variety of public records including local, state and federal tax rolls, social services lists, voter registration records and other sources. A computer is used for random selection.

The potential jurors comprise what is known as a jury pool. They are taken to the courtroom and given preliminary instructions and an introduction to the case to be tried before the presiding judge. At this stage of the proceedings, some potential jurors are excluded for extreme hardship reasons.

In some jurisdictions, potential jurors are required to fill out jury questionnaires. They are requested to provide general information about themselves, about their employment, educational background, family, hobbies, health, previous jury service and possible knowledge about the case before the court. The legal term for the process of questioning prospective jurors is "voir dire."

Eventually, names are drawn by the court-clerk and potential jurors are sealed in the courtroom. The judge then asks general questions to the jury panel. The jurors are about life experiences that could affect their impartiality.

The prosecutor and the defense attorney then ask the prospective jurors questions. Both attorneys assure the panel that they are trying to find a fair jury, when, in reality, they are both trying to find a jury that will vote with their side. Prosecutors are looking for "convictors". They are comfortable with white males and older white females. They tend to shy away from liberals, minorities, gays, strongly religious people and young women. Defense attorneys are comfortable with minorities, social workers, teachers, "artsy" people and liberals. The questions that each attorney asks are to assist them in classifying members of the panel so that each respective side knows whom they want to get rid of and whom they want to keep.

In most jurisdictions the prosecutor is given three peremptory challenges or strikes for misdemeanors and up to twenty-five for serious felonies, like murder. Peremptory challenges can be used to exclude any juror for any reason other than race, sex or sexual orientation. Prosecutors sometimes violate this rule and disguise the true reasons for using peremptory challenges to strike African-Americans. I tried a death-penalty case where the prosecutor used eleven of his first thirteen peremptory challenges to strike African-Americans, which resulted in an all-white jury.

Each side is given an unlimited number of challenges for cause. These strikes are used for potential jurors who admit that they cannot be fair, or cannot follow the law. For instance, if a potential juror's Christian beliefs prevent him or her from judging another, he or she will be challenged for the cause. A potential juror who believes that the Defendant is guilty because the police arrested him or her will be challenged for the cause.

As potential jurors are challenged, the process continues. Names are drawn and the jury box is filled with other prospective jurors who are questioned by the judge and both attorneys. Eventually, twelve jurors and two alternates are sworn in.

Many cases result in all-white juries because, more often than not, African-Americans fail to show up at the courthouse after receiving the jury summons. We do not understand or appreciate the fact that, at one time, African-Americans were not allowed to serve on juries and African-American defendants were not allowed jury trials. African-Americans must understand that our system of justice will not work if fair-minded people don't sacrifice their time and take jury duty seriously.

I have been involved in many cases where the African-Americans that did show up did everything they could to be excused from serving. Jury service can be an inconvenience because jurors have to miss work, make travel arrangements, arrange childcare, etc. Lawyers, elected officials and religious leaders have donated their time, expertise and money to fight in Washington and in the courts to ensure that our court system is fair and that we have African-Americans serving on juries. Spending a few days or weeks as a juror is a small sacrifice in comparison to the sacrifices made by those countless African-Americans who have lost their lives in war, defending this country and our constitution, as well as in the Civil Rights Movement.

I was never more frustrated in my life than I was with the excuses African-Americans made during the death penalty trial of Jonathan Parker, which was the first death penalty case tried in Buffalo, New York in over forty years. I questioned African-American schoolteachers, retirees, firemen, factory workers, welfare mothers and many others from all walks of life. I, along with other members of the defense team were trying to save Jonathan Parker's life as he was facing execution by lethal injection. An extremely high number of African-Americans from all professions and economic classes asked to be excused for hardship reasons. Each African-American that asked to be excused neglected his or her duty to ensure that a 19-year-old African-American youth had a fair trial and lost the opportunity to save a life.

It only takes one juror in a death penalty case to say no to execution, and the Defendant will, instead, receive a life sentence. Fortunately, Jonathan Parker won the fight for his life and is now serving a life sentence for the murder of a police officer. I learned after the trial that one courageous white female juror at the beginning of the deliberations in the sentencing phase boldly told the other jurors that she was not going to consider imposing the death penalty.

## The Defendant's Decision Whether or Not To Testify

The Constitution of the United States guarantees a criminal Defendant the right to remain silent. He or she does not have to testify at trial. However, a criminal Defendant has an absolute right to testify at trial if he or she chooses to. The decision whether or not to testify is a critical one. This chapter will discuss the various considerations and factors that go into an accused person's decision whether or not to testify. The right decision will make a difference in the fight for your life.

In any criminal trial the prosecutor has the burden of proving a Defendant's guilt beyond a reasonable doubt. If the prosecution fails to meet their burden of proof, then a jury must find the Defendant "not guilty". The prosecution presents their evidence first. The defense does not have to present evidence; however, if the defense does present evidence, they go last.

In most criminal trials, the Defendant is prepared to testify in advance but does not have to make a final decision until the prosecution rests its case. If a Defendant does testify on his or her own behalf, he or she will be the last witness that the jury will hear.

The first factor that a Defendant should consider concerning his or her testimony is whether or not it is needed. If the prosecution's case is weak and has holes in it, then there is a danger that the Defendant's testimony will fill in those holes and lead to a conviction. He or she then risks losing a case that was already won. If a Defendant has nothing to add to a case that has not been testified to by other witnesses, it may be a good idea to remain silent.

Any time that a witness takes the stand, his or her credibility and character become an issue. When a Defendant takes the stand, a prosecutor will cross-examine him or her about a prior criminal record and prior bad acts, subject to the judge's pre-trial ruling. A defendant with a lengthy criminal history probably should not choose to take the stand. In such a case, the jury is not likely to learn about his prior criminal history unless he takes the stand.

In all criminal cases the Judge instructs the jury that they cannot make any negative inference against a Defendant if he or she does not take the stand. Legal instructions given to jurors by the Judge makes it clear that they are not to assume that if a Defendant does not take the stand that he or she is hiding something. But, as an experienced defense attorney, I know that a large percentage of Jurors hold it against a defendant if he or she does not take the stand. If a Defendant chooses not to testify, he or she must understand that a failure to testify will have a negative impact on the jurors.

## Think Before You Act!

In many criminal trials that I have won an acquittal on, I have chosen to put my clients on the stand. To avoid the dangers of my clients hanging themselves on the stand, I spend many hours preparing them before they testify. The preparation includes familiarizing them with all statements they have given to the police or other parties in the past. I require my clients to go through several rehearsals of their examination, during which time I subject them to harsh criticism if they make any errors, have lapses in memory or get tongue-tied.

The following is a guide that will help a Defendant to be a good witness if he or she chooses to take the stand at trial.

1.  Always tell the truth. Jurors always punish the side that puts liars on the stand. In the O.J. Simpson trial, the prosecution lost primarily because their witness, Detective Mark Fuhrman was proven to be a liar. Because Fuhrman lacked credibility, the jury inferred that the whole case lacked credibility and Simpson was acquitted. If Defendants tell even a small lie, a jury may disbelieve everything they say and convict them.

2.  When you testify, look at the jury and make eye contact with them as you speak. Attorneys will be asking questions, and it will be your natural inclination to look at the person who is

asking the questions. However, it is the jury that you must convince of your innocence.

3.  Be familiar with any previous statements that you made in written or testimonial form. If there are any errors in a previous statement, be prepared to admit the mistake with a reasonable explanation.

4.  Your answers must be responsive to the question. You must listen and give a response that answers the question. There may be things that you believe are important for the jury to know; but you have to trust your attorney and believe that he or she will ask you all of the right questions to allow you to testify about important aspects of your case.

5.  When details such as times, distances, duration of events, estimates of sizes and weights are at issue, have those details worked out before you take the stand.

6.  Before you take the stand, familiarize yourself with any exhibits that will aid your testimony. You may testify about photographs, charts, diagrams or maps. If you are confused about the exhibits you testify about, you can be sure that your testimony will confuse the jury.

7.  Your defense attorney cannot ask you leading questions. Non-leading questions cannot be answered with a "yes" or "no" answer. Your attorney cannot ask you leading questions during direct examination. A leading question is a question that suggests an answer. It is objectionable for an attorney conducting a direct examination to ask the Defendant whether or not he or she was wearing a red shirt because the question is leading. It would be proper to ask, "What color was the shirt you were wearing?"

8.  When an attorney makes an objection and the judge says "over-ruled" you may answer the question.

9. When an attorney makes an objection and the judge says "sustained" you may not answer the question.

10. Your attorney, on direct examination, will try to get you to tell a story in your own words. You will be asked to tell who, why, where, when and what. You will be asked several times "What happened next?"

11. When the prosecutor asks you questions during cross-examination, do not argue with him or her. Be respectful, calm and reserved when you answer the questions.

12. Often a prosecutor will ask questions in a rapid-fire manner. You do not have to follow suit. Take your time; listen to the questions; and think about your answers before you respond.

13. Your entire testimony is recorded by a Court Reporter. Court Reporters cannot record headshakes or nods; they cannot read hand gestures; therefore, all of your responses must be verbal. Often when jurors deliberate, they ask for part of the testimony to be read back to them. There will be lapses and inaccuracies in read-backs of your testimony if it is filled with gestures and head nods.

14. You must testify in Standard English if you want to maximize your potential to get acquitted. As politically incorrect as it may sound, a Defendant who speaks Standard English will be more believable and understandable to a jury than a Defendant who speaks "Ebonics".

## Can African-Americans Receive Fair Trials from All-White Juries?

Yes, with the right attorney and the right judge, African-Americans can receive a fair trial in front of an all-white jury.

I have had dozens of trials where I successfully defended African-Americans and Hispanics in front of all-white juries; in fact, I won acquittals at two of my most recent trials. One case involved a

Hispanic male accused of raping a suburban white female. The other case involved an African-American male accused of selling drugs to a police informant.

Most people are uncomfortable discussing racial issues in public. During the jury selection process, when I have an opportunity to question prospective jurors, I am persistent in getting them to discuss the issue of race. I begin by explaining to them that most people have some degree of prejudice because of their personal experiences and the media. I illustrate to them that America is segregated on Sundays and during holidays, with Christmas being the most segregated day of the year. (Something to think about, isn't it?) Some people have the ability to set their prejudices aside and base a decision solely on the evidence. Other people assume that because the Defendant has been arrested and is Black, he or she is guilty.

## Take Note!

Here is my foolproof screening process for selecting or eliminating jurors:

▼ I get the potential jurors to examine their racial attitudes by asking them to identify minorities that they socialize with at events that are not work-related.

▼ I then ask my client to stand up and question whether they are afraid of him or her.

▼ I ask the potential jurors if they would be uncomfortable being in a room alone with my client.

▼ I then explain that they might have a right to be prejudiced. However, if their prejudice is so strong that they feel my client did something wrong before they have heard any evidence, then maybe they should not serve on this case.

> ▼ If their prejudice interferes in any way with their ability to be impartial in evaluating the evidence, and they cannot afford him or her the presumption of innocence, they should not sit on the jury.
>
> ▼ I ask them to discuss any negative experiences that they have had with African-Americans and how those experiences would affect their ability to be impartial.
>
> ▼ I ask them to describe the racial attitudes of their parents and how the attitudes of their parents shaped their attitudes on race.

A Racist is a person who is prejudiced and uses his or her power to treat a minority unfairly. I instruct the potential jurors that if they serve on the jury and let their prejudice interfere with their evaluation of the evidence, they are racists. A Racist Jury is wrong and harms all people in our society.

After hearing my speech and instructions, many prospective jurors have raised their hands and requested to be excused. Those that remain are sensitive to their own racial attitudes and, at least, will attempt to look at the evidence and disregard the race of the defendant. Furthermore, after closely examining the jurors' attitudes on race, I can use my peremptory challenges to excuse those who I believe were lying to me and cannot be fair.

Some judges will create an atmosphere in the courtroom where jurors are encouraged to speak openly about racial attitudes. Some judges will liberally grant challenges for cause when it is clear that a potential juror's racial bias would affect his or her ability to be impartial. On the other hand, some judges limit the attorneys questioning of the jury panel on racial attitudes. They attempt to rehabilitate jurors who have indicated under oath that they cannot be fair by convincing them that they can set aside their bias. With these types of judges, there is no way a minority can get a fair trial before an all-white jury.

I have witnessed many trials where the defense attorneys are not skilled enough or smart enough, or do not care enough to question prospective jurors about race. As a result of the defense attorney's ineffectiveness in failing to properly question the jurors about their racial attitudes, there is a lasting danger that many African-Americans have been and will be wrongfully convicted.

Now that you know more about the jury selection process, discuss it thoroughly with your attorney and use your insight to your advantage. If the search for African-American jurors fails and you find that most of the jurors assigned to your trial are white, hopefully, your attorney has fully examined the jurors on racial bias and those that are unfit have been excused.

## CRIME REPORT: "PREDOMINANTLY WHITE JURY SPARES AFRICAN-AMERICAN MALE'S LIFE"

Jonathan Parker is described as a 20-year-old street criminal. He was 19 when he shot a police officer. At the age of 20, he was convicted of first-degree murder.

The Governor had attended the police officer's funeral; it turned out to be a political trial. Governor Pataki previously removed a District Attorney in another county from a case who did not seek the death penalty in the murder of a police officer. Pataki was elected, in part, on a promise to restore the death penalty in New York State. I had the feeling that the death penalty was being sought to use Parker as a political example/sacrifice. Fortunately, for Parker, the jurors didn't want to see injustice served; they didn't want to see another killing of a disadvantaged youth out of revenge for the murder of a police officer. In order for the sentence to be either death or life in prison, the jurors would have had to vote unanimously.

Under the New York State's capital punishment law, the judge had been required to ask each of the seven women and five men on the jury, as well as the four female and three male alternates if their views on capital punishment had changed since the trial began. After delivering a verdict of guilty, the jurors received raucous courthouse applause from dozens of officers as the panel left the courtroom.

I, along with other members of the defense team, then had to prepare for the penalty phase of trial which would determine whether our client would be executed or sentenced to jail for the rest of his life.

## Always Remember...

If you don't have the funds to hire the most experienced criminal attorney, don't let racism block your right to a fair trial.

## Chapter Seven
# Cooperating With the Government: The Snitch

On September 28, 1994 Sammy "The Bull" Gravano was sentenced to five years in prison followed by three years of supervised release because of his cooperation with the Federal Government that led to the conviction of several key members of organized crime families, including John Gotti. Sammy "The Bull" was a Mafia "hit man" (executioner) who participated in nineteen murders, including the murder of former Gambino crime family boss Paul Castellano. Gravano was facing a potential life sentence, if convicted on conspiracy and racketeering charges. He served only five years in prison on racketeering charges. Sammy "The Bull" won the fight for his life by cooperating with the government.

A cooperating informant, sometimes referred to as a "Snitch", "Stool Pigeon", or "Rat" is someone who receives a benefit from law enforcement officials in exchange for their cooperation. Cooperating informants are sometimes paid money for their work, but most often, they are rewarded with a plea bargain that gives them reduced jail time, and in some instances, a dismissal of the charges. The cooperation provided by the informant may be in the form of testimony.

Cooperation may also include active participation in law enforcement, such as setting up drug deals, or wearing surveillance devices to obtain incriminating information.

Not all cooperating witnesses win the fight for their lives the way Sammy "The Bull" did. In fact, some informants have been injured or killed, or their family members have been injured or killed in retaliation for their public service.

I represented "Manuel" in a major narcotics possession case. Manuel was caught with a quantity of cocaine that could have put him in jail for twenty-five years to life. He was from New Jersey; and I suspected that he went from city to city selling drugs for a short period of time and then moved on before he became well known to the police. Manuel's wife posted $10,000.00 cash bail to get him released from custody after his arrest.

Manuel was streetwise and knew that if he agreed to make a deal early on, he would receive a favorable treatment from prosecutors. Within a week of his release from jail, Manuel became a police informant. Approximately five months after his arrest, he came to my office complaining about the narcotics detectives being too demanding. He told me that no matter how hard he worked for the detectives, they were never satisfied. Before he left my office, I agreed to schedule a meeting with the prosecutor and detectives to address his concerns.

The very next day, I opened the morning paper and read that Manuel was the victim of a homicide. No one was ever arrested for his murder. I suspect that he was killed because people in the drug world that he was associated with, found out what he was up to. I spoke to the detectives that he was working with and they, of course, denied that his death was the result of undercover activities.

Manuel's wife called me and didn't seem particularly upset about the murder. At her request, I made arrangements to have the bail money released. She flew to Buffalo and we had a brief meeting in my office.

She signed the papers to have the bail money released to her; I never heard from her again. Manuel's murder received little news coverage, and to this day, remains unsolved. Manuel lost the fight for his life, and no one seemed to care.

Cooperating witnesses must never disclose what they are doing to anyone, even their closest family members. Another time, I represented "Julie", who decided to work with police after being busted for drugs. She was told not to discuss what she was doing with anyone, including her family. Her brother, reportedly, was involved in drug trafficking; and the detectives were concerned that if her brother became aware that she was cooperating, she would no longer be useful as an informant because her brother would compromise her. Julie had a very close relationship with her mother. She eventually told her mother, who promised not to tell anyone. Of course, Mom broke her promise and told her son.

Soon after, Julie went out dancing at a popular club on a Saturday evening. She was attacked and severely beaten by two women. Julie was taken to the emergency room of a local hospital, where she received 140 stitches to her face. She now has a scar, stretching from ear to ear, across her cheek to the corner of her mouth. (Many inmates bear similar scars from attacks made on them in retaliation for snitching while in prison.) Julie couldn't keep a secret; her mother couldn't keep a secret; and her brother wouldn't keep a secret. If it weren't for skilled emergency physicians, Julie would have lost the fight for her life.

I have, fortunately, represented informants who were luckier than Manuel and Julie. One of my clients was caught with several kilograms of cocaine. His cooperation led to the arrest of several major drug dealers. Because of his cooperation, my client, who was facing life imprisonment, never spent a single day in jail. I have represented many others who have avoided jail or earned substantially reduced sentencing because of their cooperation.

From time to time, I am called upon to defend people charged in drug cases, who were set up by informants. I have learned that sometimes informants will lie, plant drugs on people, and perjure themselves under oath. "Sam", a 35-year-old African-American co-owner of a sub shop, recently hired me. Sam was arrested for, and charged with selling $300.00 of crack cocaine to an informant. If convicted, Sam would have received a life sentence, because he had two prior felony convictions. After trial, the all-white jury deliberated 1½ hours and found Sam "not guilty". The Jury believed my argument and Sam's testimony that he was set up by the informant. At trial, the Jury learned that Sam had had an affair with the informant's 16-year-old sister, who became pregnant and had an abortion. The informant had been employed by Sam and got fired: he owed Sam quite a bit of money.

I spoke with the jurors after the trial and they believed that the informant had hidden drugs on his person, and then had gone to Sam under the guise of repaying the loan. They also believed that informant then gave police the crack cocaine and falsely claimed he had gotten it from Sam. My client, Sam, won the fight for his life and now lives with his wife and two children.

Personally, I do not like informant testimony, because there is a danger that innocent people will end up being convicted.

I have sat in a number of meetings with prosecutors and clients who were informants. Typically, during these meetings, before anything is said, a prosecutor tells the informant what his investigation had revealed, based on what the informant knows and what benefits would be given in exchange for testimony. The informant then just repeats everything that the prosecutor told him about the investigation. It would seem that a clever, cooperating witness would want to please the prosecutor, even if it meant telling lies; the happier the prosecutor is, the less jail time the informant will receive.

After these factors have been taken into consideration, it may be determined whether the snitch's testimony is admissible at the trial.

# FYI...The Cooperating Informant

To protect the criminal justice system from infiltrating false or unreliable testimony from jailhouse informers into a trial, it is important for the defense attorney to obtain as much information about the informant as possible, including:

▼ Records and receipts of any monetary consideration that the information was received in exchange for his cooperation.

▼ The complete criminal history of the informer.

▼ List of any deals, promises, considerations or benefits that the informant has been offered for his or her testimony.

▼ What the defendant allegedly stated to the informant and the time, place and circumstances of those statements.

▼ Lists of any other cases the informant has been involved in and all benefits received from those involvements.

▼ Notes on whether the informant has ever changed his or her testimony or lied during court proceedings.

▼ Transcripts of the informant's testimony in all other cases.

▼ Notes of all police and prosecution interviews of the informants.

If you are arrested for serious criminal charges, and wish to cooperate with the police and prosecutors, the following rules should apply:

1. Hire an attorney before any deals are reached, and before any cooperation begins. An experienced criminal defense attorney will make sure that you are treated fairly and that you will get full credit for your cooperation.

2. The earlier a Defendant begins to cooperate, the better deal he or she gets.

3. Be reliable.

4. Do not discuss cooperation with anyone except the police, prosecutor and your attorney. Being a cooperating witness or informant is dangerous. If people find out you are a "snitch", you will no longer be able to effectively gather information because you have been exposed. Also, by telling people what you are doing, you may be placing your life, or the lives of your loved ones, in danger of a possible retaliation.

5. Do not engage in any criminal activity. If you are arrested while you are cooperating, you will be dropped from the program.

6. Do not use narcotics while you are a cooperating witness or informant. If you fail a drug test, your credibility as a witness will be tarnished and you may be dropped from the program.

7. Understand that prosecutors, and not police officers, have the final say in the disposition of your case. Police officers make recommendations to prosecutors, but they do not have the authority to dismiss charges or offer plea bargains.

8. Understand that detectives are very busy. If you are a cooperating informant working with a detective, it is up to you to keep in contact with the detective. Do not wait for him or her.

9. If you change your telephone number or address, notify your attorney and the detective assigned to your case.

10. Your cooperation will be evaluated on results, not effort. A "nice try" that doesn't result in an arrest, conviction or seizure of contraband will get you nothing.

## The Jailhouse Informer

In a recent homicide case, a man was accused of murdering his next-door neighbors. The prosecutor had taken the testimony of a jailhouse informer (snitch), which stated that the defendant had allegedly admitted killing the victims. He also allegedly told the snitch about some of the facts surrounding the killings, and the reasons why the state would have a hard time proving the case.

The informer stuck with his story during the preliminary hearing, but then recanted it during the trial. His credibility was already lacking when the defendant's attorney uncovered information about two letters the snitch had written—one telling investigators that he expected favorable treatment and the other telling the prosecutor that he no longer had to lie for them, implying there really had been no confession from the defendant.

## CRIME REPORT:
## ADMITTING FALSE TESTIMONY? AT WHAT COST?

Sometimes, more often than not, innocent people get trapped in a plot to catch a scapegoat. Police or prosecutors may decide that it's time to close a case, and find someone who is willing to "cash in" by submitting false testimony. Former criminals, rapists, con artists, murderers and perjurers have been known to become snitches for the right price.

One such case involved a $250,000 payoff to a former cop, deep in debt, alcohol and drugs, who was asked to set up a sting operation to catch Latin American drug smugglers. Having obtained false evidence of a crime, the snitch involved an unknowing party in an illegal operation and, based on false testimony, caused that party's conviction.

Another case involved a college student who was a promising athlete. He was paid $1500 to drive some friends to a make drug deal. Later, when they got caught, those so-called friends were given the option of snitching or getting a life sentence—they snitched on their driver. Although he had no prior record, the college student, got three life terms for driving the car. Three of his snitches got reduced sentences and one even got acquitted.

(Source: *The Champion*—"*Twisted Justice: Prosecution Function in America Out of Control*" by Jack King)

## Always Remember...

Defense attorneys cannot pay witnesses to testify, but prosecutors are allowed to give informants money, and even their freedom, in exchange for their testimony.

*"Before I ride with a drunk,*
*I'll drive myself."*
—Stevie Wonder

## Chapter Eight
# Driving While Intoxicated Can Alter Your Life...Forever

According to statistics provided by the National Highway Association, in 2002, 17, 400 people in the United States were killed in motor vehicle accidents involving alcohol. An average of one person every minute is injured in accidents where alcohol is involved. A drunk driver kills someone every thirty minutes.

Since 1979, I have seen how drunk drivers have ruined the lives of innocent people, themselves and their own families. As a New York State Trooper, I arrested many drunk drivers. Oftentimes I was the first person at the scene of a drunk-driving accident fatality. As an attorney, I have prosecuted and defended many people accused of drunk driving.

### Think Before You Act!!

When you get into a car under the influence of alcohol, you do not intend to cause harm; but little do you know that when you turn on the ignition to the car, you are about to enter the "Twilight Zone". Driving while intoxicated is a crime.

A few years ago, I represented a woman in her early 20's. She was the mother of two young children and had lived a quiet and peaceful life with her family. She had attended a wedding reception and had quite a bit to drink; then made the mistake of attempting to drive home.

While traveling down a dimly lit road, my client heard a loud "THUMP" and lost control of her SUV. When the vehicle came to a halt, a nightmare became a reality. Four people who had left the same wedding reception were walking along the shoulder of the road, and were struck, then dragged by the SUV, leaving carnage along the roadside. A young woman who, up to that point, had lived a law-abiding life was now a Defendant in a quadruple homicide.

I had never seen a client in as much mental distress and pain. At her sentencing, I told the judge how my client would have gladly given her own life in exchange for the lives of those killed in the accident. I also told the Court about her concern for her two young children, who would be raised without a mother while she was incarcerated.

She was sentenced to serve four years in jail. Her life, the lives of her children, and the lives of the victims' families will never be the same. My hope is that all who read this will never drink and drive. I always tell my clients who have been arrested for Driving While Intoxicated that they need to seek help for a drinking problem. Anytime you are arrested and alcohol is a factor in the arrest, you have a drinking problem.

## FYI...Counseling & Support

Sometimes, a few counseling sessions might be all that are needed; other times, long-term inpatient care may be required. Alcoholics Anonymous has support groups located in most communities; many churches offer support and counseling for people with drinking problems, as well.

For those of you who choose not to heed my advice and happen to get arrested for DUI/DWI, I will explain some of the legal formalities that will occur and your legal rights.

When a police officer questions a person suspected of Driving While Under the Influence of alcohol, he is looking for certain signs that will determine whether there is probable cause for an arrest. Typical signs of intoxication are slurred speech, an odor of alcohol, poor balance or motor coordination and bloodshot eyes. The officer will question the driver about the number of drinks the suspect has consumed and where he or she is going.

If the officer notices that the suspect driver has some of the signs of intoxication, he will ask the driver to perform a series of field sobriety tests, including: reading the alphabet, walking and turning, standing on one leg, and touching the tip of the index finger to the tip of the nose. If the suspect fails to perform well on these tests, he or she will be placed under arrest.

After placing a driver under arrest for Driving While Intoxicated, the suspect is advised of his or her Miranda Rights and taken to the police station for booking. Within two hours, the suspect is given further warnings about submitting to a breath test, or blood test to determine the level of alcohol contained in the suspect's blood. The driver may refuse to take the test, or he or she may consent to the test. In certain cases involving an accident where there is a serious injury or fatality, the officer can get a court order for a forced blood test if the driver refuses.

If questioned by police when suspected of drunk driving, the motorist should be aware that anything they do or say can and will be used against him or her in court. Miranda Rights are not required to be read to a suspect unless they are placed under arrest in a traffic stop situation. So, if a driver admits to having three or four drinks while the officer is investigating whether he or she is drunk, the admission that they were drinking will be used against them at trial.

The performance of a motorist on the field sobriety test will be used against them at trial, even if they were not read their Miranda Rights.

If questioned by the police, the suspect has the right to consult with an attorney and refuse field sobriety tests. If a motorist asks for an attorney, the police must stop questioning him or her until an attorney gives permission to continue questioning.

At many police stations, the booking areas are under video surveillance with hidden cameras. I have represented many people who insisted that they were falsely arrested for driving while intoxicated until they saw how foolish and "sloppy drunk" they appeared on the video.

## Take Note...

The legal standard for Driving While Intoxicated is .08% Blood Alcohol Content. For example, if a 150-pound man were to consume three drinks in one hour, he would fail the test. Coffee and exercise do not reduce the level of intoxication; time does reduce the level of intoxication. Alcohol leaves the body at the rate of about one drink per hour for the average person.

In most states, if a motorist is requested to take a blood or breath test and he or she refuses, there are serious consequences. At trial, most courts will instruct the jury that the motorist's refusal to take a blood or breath test can be used as evidence that he or she was intoxicated. Many states will suspend driving privileges of a motorist who refuses to take a blood or breath test, even if he or she is acquitted of Driving While Intoxicated.

Some prosecutors have plea policies that preclude making a plea offer to a reduced charge for motorists who refuse to take the test.

In most cases, I believe that a motorist should take a blood or alcohol test, if requested. Sometimes, the results of the test can exonerate the driver. Such was the case of an 80-year-old school bus driver who I successfully defended. He had appeared to be intoxicated, but was simply over-medicated. In my opinion, a refusal is simply not worth the consequences of a license suspension or the denial of a reduced plea.

However, in some cases, a motorist should refuse the test. If there is a fatality or serious physical injury, or if the motorist is charged with a felony, a refusal may make sense. The best policy concerning taking or refusing to take a blood or breath test is to speak to an attorney first, because each case is different and your decision could adversely and seriously effect your case.

**DO NOT DRINK AND DRIVE.** It isn't worth it to your health and safety, and the health and safety of other innocent people. A conviction for Driving While Intoxicated can result in a jail sentence, a heavy fine, suspension of driving privileges, and a denial of auto insurance coverage. If you are driving while intoxicated and have a serious car accident, there may be no need for you to hire a criminal defense attorney because you will be dead and will have lost the Fight for Your Life.

CRIME REPORT:
"DEATH ON A NEW JERSEY HIGHWAY"

After a night of boozing it up in New Jersey strip clubs a man was pulled over with more than twice the legal limit of alcohol in his system. He called a friend to take him home after the state police had arrested him; but instead the friend drove him back to his car. The drunk driver was at the wheel of the car that caused a fatal accident—which killed him as well as another man and critically injured a woman in the second car.

The "Friend" was charged with manslaughter, vehicular homicide and aggravated assault by auto in a collision that killed two people and critically injured a third person. He wasn't in either of the cars involved in the crash, yet he faced 15 years in prison if convicted. The seven-man, five-woman jury in the landmark case of a New Jersey man charged as an accessory to murder for letting his best friend drive drunk was not able to reach a verdict, and the judge declared a mistrial.

(Source: CBSNEWS.COM)

## Always Remember...

The first place you should go to get help for an alcohol problem is your personal physician, who will then refer you to a clinic where you can be evaluated as to the extent of treatment that is needed.

*"Father only means that you are taking care of your children. That's what it means to be a father. It doesn't mean having babies. Anybody can make a baby, but a father helps to raise his children. There is another word for fatherhood. It's called responsibility"*
—Malcolm X

## Chapter Nine
# Sex Crimes and Date Rape

One out of every six American women has been the victim of an attempted or completed rape in her lifetime. Every two minutes, somewhere in America, someone is sexually assaulted. Between 1995 and 1996, more than 670,000 women were the victims of rape, attempted rape or sexual assault. In 2001, there were 249,000 victims of rape, attempted rape and sexual assault. It has been reported that about 18% of those rape victims are African-American. Those from low-income households income are twice as likely to be victims of a sexual assault; and, unfortunately many of these victims feel like rape is their fault. *(Source: www.rainn.org/ statistics.html)*

I suspect that the reported percentages might be low for this crime because, for centuries (beginning with slavery) African-American women have been raped and it has, unfortunately, been considered just another part of life.

## Rape Defined

Rape occurs when sex is non-consensual (not agreed upon), or a person forces another person to have sex against his or her will. It also can occur when the victim is intoxicated from alcohol or drugs (such as Ecstasy). Rape includes intercourse in the vagina, anus, or mouth. It is a felony offense, which means it is among the most serious crimes a person can commit. Men as well as women and children can be raped.

Many times, the person who commits rape uses violence to force the person to have sex. An attacker also can use fear alone to commit rape. Rape causes both physical and emotional harm to the victim.

"Date" rape also occurs when one person forces another person to have sex; and it, too, is a felony offense. The difference between rape and date rape is that the victim agreed to spend time with the attacker. Perhaps he or she even went out with his or her attacker more than once.

Statutory rape is having sex with a person who is to young to legally consent to have sex. In most states, if you have sex with a female under the age of sixteen, you will find yourself in big trouble. It doesn't matter if she's fifteen, but looks and acts twenty-one.

## Date Rape—A Growing Concern for the Young Black Male

A lot of young African-American males do not understand that when a woman says "no" to sex "NO" means "NO". Rape is a violent crime. In most states, rape convictions require mandatory imprisonment. Sexual offenders are required to register by law with state authorities on sexual offender registration lists for life. You also need to understand that a lack of knowledge of the age of the victim is not a defense to Statutory rape charges. In most states, the age of consent is seventeen.

80

## Think Before You Act...
## Loose Lips Sink Ships

When a young man has sex with a young woman, he should respect her and keep their personal business to himself. Bragging about your sexual conquest can lead to false allegations of rape.

I once represented a university engineering student. He left a party with a coed and had consensual sex. The next day, he bragged about his sexual conquest and talked about how nasty the young lady was. When she heard the rumors that were spreading across the college she went to campus security and reported that she had been raped.

The engineering student was arrested and charged with rape. At the trial I was able to demonstrate to the jury that there was no evidence of force. In a typical rape case, the medical records will indicate vaginal tears, bruises to the inner thighs, and bruising to the arms where the victim was held down. Due to the lack of evidence of force, the jury believed my client's testimony over the alleged rape victim.

However, my client suffered serious consequences as a result of his arrest. He spent a week in jail before his out-of-town father could come to post bail. University authorities threw him out of the college dormitory, because he was a possible danger to female students. College administration suspended him from college for a year; and his parents footed a legal bill that cost several thousand dollars.

I had another recent trial where one of my clients was accused of date rape. While at a backyard "keg" party, Jose and his friend had sex with a very intoxicated girl in the basement of the home. After having sex, Jose bragged to his friends that "he just "f——ed some bitch and she was down in the basement naked." When the girl's friends went to the basement, they discovered her highly intoxicated, confused and disorientated.

Jose was accused of rape. If convicted at trial, Jose would have been sent to prison for 12 ½ to 23 years. He turned down a plea bargain that would have sent him away for three years. Fortunately, there were several witnesses who saw the girl kissing and fondling Jose and his friend Joe before going into the basement. Ultimately, Jose was found to be not guilty. His friend was not charged because there was no DNA evidence linking him to the sexual encounter. (I suspect that Jose's friend used a condom and that Jose did not.)

Never have sex with a stranger; it will only lead to trouble; just ask Kobe Bryant or Mike Tyson.

I successfully represented Charles, a brilliant young African-American man who was a computer wizard. Unfortunately, because of his computer wizardry, he ended up in a chat room and met a white girl. He went over to her parent's home and they had sex; when the parents found out, the consensual sex became a rape. Charles was arrested.

In New York State, charges are presented to a Grand Jury in felony cases. A Grand Jury is composed of 23 people and they hear evidence in secret. The prosecutor presents evidence to the grand Jury and acts as a legal advisor. Twelve of the twenty-three Grand Jurors must vote to indict or the charges are dismissed. I made a tactical decision to allow the "Computer Wiz" to testify before the Grand Jury. The alleged victim testified two or three weeks before Charles. I delayed Charles from testifying as long as I could.

When I accompanied "The Computer Wiz" to the Grand Jury, I noticed that there were only sixteen Grand Jurors present. In order for the Grand Jury to dismiss the charges, "The Computer Wiz" only had to convince five of the sixteen Grand Jurors that there was not probable cause of rape because it requires twelve votes for indictment. The "Computer Wiz" was facing the fight of his life because he was facing a potential sentence of 25 years, if convicted. At least five of the Grand Jurors believed the "Computer Wiz" because the charges were dismissed.

It should be understood that, because of significant disadvantages, a defendant will testify in the Grand Jury in only a very small percentage of criminal cases. Neither the defendant nor his attorney is present in the Grand Jury when other evidence is presented. The defense attorney does not have an opportunity to question the defendant, who is only asked questions by the prosecutor and the Grand Jurors. If there is an indictment, the prosecutor can use the transcript of your Grand Jury testimony against you at the trial.

I would never have asked the "Computer Wiz" to testify before the Grand Jury if he did not have extreme intellect and had not spent numerous hours preparing to testify.

## Statutory Rape—Is She Too Young to Consent?

I recently represented "Miles", an African-American man, who found out the hard way that lack of knowledge of the age of your sexual partner is no defense to statutory rape charges. "Miles" was a twenty-year-old high school graduate, with one semester of community college credit under his belt. He worked full-time, making a decent salary. He was a neat dresser, and a polite, respectful young man. One hot summer evening, Miles received a call from his cousin, and was invited to hang out with him and two girls, who happened to be white. Eventually, they went to Miles' apartment to watch movies. They drank some liquor, and before the evening was over, both couples ended up having sex in the living room.

Miles' date told him that she was eighteen years old, and living with her parents. She acted like she was eighteen, and he had no reason to believe otherwise.

After an evening of booze and sex, his date became very drunk and passed out. He revived her by splashing water on her face and forced her to drink coffee. Miles then took her to her parents' home; and

83

they called the police. Eventually, the girl was taken to the emergency room and examined for a possible rape; whereupon the doctors determined that she had had unprotected sex.

Miles was arrested and charged with felony statutory rape. He was facing the possibility of seven years in prison. I was eventually able to get the charges reduced to a misdemeanor and kept Miles out of jail with a sentence of probation.

All states now keep public records of people who are convicted of sex crimes on a Sexual Offenders Registration List. The names of people on the list are available to the public on the Internet and at police stations. Sexual offenders must report any address changes to the police, who distribute lists to the schools and neighbors close to the most serious sexual offenders….Miles name is now included on this list.

## Take Note!
## Doing Drugs Can Lead To Date Rape

If a person has had too much to drink or is on drugs they cannot consent to sex and having sex with them is legally rape. Although girls are more often victims of rape, guys are not "safe"—they can be raped too.

"Date Rape" drugs may be difficult to trace but evidence of intercourse is not, and in cases where use of these drugs is suspected, evidence of rape standards are lower. Certain "date rape" drugs render the victim unconscious and limit memory; using these drugs on somebody is not actually "date rape" but a federal crime with a possible 20-year sentence.

*(See: 1996 Drug-Induced Rape Prevention and Punishment Act)*
*(Source: http://teenadvice.about.com/library/bl10thingsdaterape.htm)*

# Club Drugs Can Ruin Your Life...Forever

*(Source: Know The Dangers of Ecstasy and Other Club Drugs—Channing Bete Company)*

There are many dangers associated with using drugs. Some may be more familiar to you than others, because they have been available for a longer time; but all that are listed here are considered "Club Drugs". Using them can lead to violence, date rape, imprisonment and even death; there's no way to know what their ingredients are or how much of an ingredient they contain.

Some of the many reasons why you might decide to use club drugs are to escape your problems, to experiment, or to feel like part of a crowd (peer pressure among teens has been known to cause irreparable harm). You should, however, rely on your instinct to survive.

Avoiding club drugs could save your life; they can harm your judgment and place you in a situation from which there is no escape. In addition, drug dependency is a major threat to your future and could even involve you in situations that could land you in jail.

▼ Marijuana affects thinking and behavior; and long-term usage can lead to lung disease.

▼ Methamphetamine or "meth" is a stimulant that can cause depression, seizures and stroke.

▼ LSD or "acid" is a hallucinogen that can cause distorted perceptions, increased heart rate and other problems, which can ultimately lead to death.

▼ Cocaine is a highly addictive stimulant, which can cause seizures, heart attacks, coma and death.

▼ Inhalants are harmful chemicals, such as: amyl and butyl nitrite (poppers) or nitrous oxide (whippets) that can cause heart problems, brain damage and sudden death.

▼ Alcohol is also considered a club drug, especially if it is mixed with other drugs.

▼ Ecstasy is one of the most widely used club drugs. It acts as both a stimulant, which can speed up the central nervous system and a hallucinogen, which affects thinking, awareness and the senses. Ecstasy, also known as: XTC, and essence. Can cause anxiety or panic, nausea or loss of appetite, chills, sweating or fainting, distorted thoughts, feelings or aware-ness, and increased heart rate and blood pressure. Because ingredients can vary widely, effects are very unpredictable; when combined with intense physical activity, Ecstasy can cause overheating, which can lead to kidney failure and death.

▼ Herbal Ecstasy is a stimulant, which unfortunately, has been passed off as a safe alternative to ecstasy. Other names used have been X, Herbal X, Cloud 9 and Ultimate Xphoria. The main ingredient in Herbal Ecstasy is a stimulant called ephed-rine, which is used to treat asthma and nasal congestion.

▼ Rohypnol and GHB are depressants, which slow down the central nervous system. Rohypnol is also known as: roach, rope or the forget pill, it is used in other countries medically to treat insomnia and anxiety. GHB is also known as: Liquid X, scoop or Georgia Home Boy; and has been used in Europe as an anesthetic. Some side effects of Rohypnol and GHB include: drowsiness, confusion, dizziness and head-ache, impaired judgment, difficulty speaking and walking, and amnesia and/or loss of consciousness—in many instances a date rape victim may not remember the incident.

▼ Ketamine is an anesthetic, which also acts as a hallucinogen (anesthetics dull pain). Also known as: K, Special K, Vita-min K, Super K and New Ecstasy, Ketamine is used as a sur-gical anesthetic for animals. It can cause numbness, lack of coordination, raised blood pressure, vomiting, distorted thoughts and depression. The effects of this drug are very unpredictable, as they have resulted in delirium, seizures and even violent behavior.

Serious health problems have resulted from the use of club drugs, including: seizures, coma, heart attack or stroke, overdose and death. Many young and unsuspecting women have become victims of date rate because club drugs have been "slipped" into their drinks. Some are difficult to detect because they are odorless and colorless. This is a serious crime, which should be reported to the police; if convicted of using these drugs to perform date rape, the defendant may be fined and sentenced to several years in prison.

If you suspect that you are in an environment where club drugs are readily available, you must stay alert and avoid taking any drinks from strangers; just say "no". If you feel uncomfortable with a situation, leave immediately (even if you have to call your parents to pick you up).

Call 911 or your local emergency number if you become suddenly sick, get confused, or pass out after taking a drink—you may have been drugged.

## What You Should Do If You Have Been Raped

If you have been sexually assaulted, get to a safe place as soon as you are able. If you aren't sure if what happened to you was rape, a rape crisis counselor or doctor can help you sort it out.

▼ Call the police and tell them what happened. If you are afraid to call the police, call your local rape crisis center. (Carry this number in your wallet with other emergency numbers)

▼ Don't wash or douche. You do not want to wash away any evidence that could be used against your attacker in court.

▼ Go to an emergency room to be examined. A doctor will make a record of your injuries and treat you. Samples of any fluid left in the vagina or anus (especially semen) will be gathered. Hair, pieces of clothing or other objects left by the attacker also may be taken. These samples may be used to help identify and convict your attacker.

## FYI...Statistics

*(Provided by Violence against Women & National Crime Victimization Survey and Bureau of Justice Statistics, U.S. Department of Justice)*

The numbers of unreported sex crimes is startling; most victims believe that it is a private or personal matter and they fear reprisal from the assailant.

▼ Approximately 84% of rapes and sexual assaults go unreported to law enforcement officials.

▼ Approximately 85% of rape victims knew their assailant.

▼ Approximately 28% of victims are raped by husbands or boyfriends; 35% by acquaintances; and 5% by other relatives.

▼ A survivor of sexual assault is nine times more likely than the average person to attempt suicide.

▼ The average rapist rapes between eight and sixteen women before he is caught.

▼ Teens 16 to 19 were three and one-half times more likely than the general population to be victims of rape, attempted rape or sexual assault; and approximately one-third of all juvenile victims of sexual abuse cases are children younger than 6 years of age.

▼ Date Rape is the most common form of rape (78%) with 1 in 4 girls expected to fall victim to rape or attempted rape before they reach 25, and 3 out of 5 rapes occurring before a woman reaches age 18.

(Source: Rape Statistics)

## How, When and Where Rape By a Stranger Usually Occurs

Many ex-convicts who may have been minor offenders before being incarcerated have become more serious dangers to society because of sexual assaults made on them by other inmates. Many of them have become the strangers that prey on innocent and unsuspecting female rape victims, which result in repeated and uncontrollable violent attacks, and far too often, in murder.

These are some of the facts:

▼ One of every four rapes takes place in a public area or in a parking garage.

▼ 29% of female victims reported that the offender was a stranger.

▼ 68% of rapes occur between the hours of 6 p.m. and 6 a.m.

▼ At least 45% of rapists were under the influence of alcohol or drugs.

▼ In 29% of rapes, the offender used a weapon

▼ In 47% of rapes, the victim sustained injuries other than rape injuries

▼ 75% of female rape victims require medical care after the attack.

CRIME REPORT:
"MAN ACQUITTED IN 2-YEAR-OLD RAPE CASE"

One of my clients, a twenty-three year old man, was acquitted of raping a former girlfriend at his mother's home.

At the close of a five-day trial, after two hours of deliberations, a jury found the defendant innocent of single counts of first-degree rape, first-degree sodomy, first-degree sex abuse and third degree robbery.

I represented the same man for an incident involving a sixteen-year-old girl. He was acquitted of first-degree forcible rape and sodomy; however, the jury convicted him of rape and sodomy in the third degree because she was under-age.

## Always Remember...

Always go out in groups and look out for each other; never walk alone to your car or go off alone with a stranger; trust your instincts.

*"The ultimate weakness of violence is that it is a descending spiral, begetting the very thing it seeks to destroy. Instead of diminishing evil, it multiplies it....Through violence you may murder the hater, but you do not murder hate. In fact, violence merely increases hate... Returning violence for violence multiplies violence, adding deeper darkness to a night already devoid of stars. Darkness cannot drive out hate; only love can do that.*
—**Reverend Dr. Martin Luther King, Jr.**

## Chapter Ten
# Does the Crime Fit the Punishment?

As a defense attorney, I investigate and evaluate every case and give my clients an assessment of the evidence against them. In cases where that evidence is overwhelming, I make a recommendation that the case be resolved with a plea bargain. When the evidence against my client is weak, I will make a recommendation that the case proceed to trial. My recommendations are strictly made based upon the evidence, and not actual innocence or guilt. I know that in our justice system sometimes the juries acquit people who have committed crimes and convict people who have not committed crimes.

### Plea Bargaining: Know When to Hold Them and When to Fold Them

Over 90% of criminal cases are resolved by plea-bargains. A plea-bargain is a plea of guilty to a reduced charge, or a plea of guilty to the charge in exchange for a lesser sentence. A common example of a plea-bargain is when a person who is charged with shoplifting and facing a year in jail agrees to plea to a non-criminal charge of disorderly conduct with a $250.00 fine as agreed upon sentence. The prosecution benefits from the plea-bargain process because they can use resources to prosecute more serious crimes and a case is resolved. The judge is happy to have a case removed from his heavy caseload. The Defendant is happy to have avoided a long jail sentence.

One of the problems with plea-bargaining is that, sometimes, innocent people are found guilty of crimes that they did not commit because they cannot afford to make bail. This happens very often in local criminal courts on misdemeanor cases. A good example would be of a young man, who cannot afford bail; he has been accused of a minor theft or drug case that he did not commit and is offered a sentence of time served if he pleads guilty. Rather than wait several weeks or months in jail while awaiting trial, the defendant will use his common sense and plead guilty to the crime so that he can be released from custody, be with his family, and not be fired from his job.

The issue of innocent people pleading guilty is more problematic in death penalty cases. Imagine a person accused of a crime he did not commit who is facing death by lethal injection. Eyewitnesses to the murder have mistakenly identified the defendant as the killer. The defendant lives alone and has no one to verify his alibi. The prosecutor offers the defendant a life sentence if he pleads guilty. What does the defendant do? Does he go to trial to save his life and plead to a crime he did not commit, knowing he will spend the rest of his life in jail?

Our system of justice is not perfect. In 2000, Illinois Governor George Ryan issued a moratorium on the death penalty in that state due to mounting evidence that innocent people were convicted, and sentenced to death. It has been proven that since the death penalty was re-imposed in Illinois, twelve innocent people were executed, and thirteen were freed from death row.

Knowing when to accept a plea bargain and when to reject one is like being a good poker player; you must "know when to hold them and when to fold them". I have a former client who I advised to accept a plea bargain; he fired me after my "strong" urging and is now serving a 57-year sentence. The client was arrested for breaking and entering into an elderly woman's home, then raping and sodomizing her. Eyewitnesses saw my client running from the scene of the crime. The elderly woman positively identified him in open court during the pre-trial hearings. DNA evidence confirmed that my client's semen was present; medical records indicated that the victim suffered vaginal trauma consistent with rape.

Before my former client hired me, there was a plea offer of thirty years. After I was hired, I obtained a court ruling from the judge that required the victim's testimony at a hearing before trial. Because of my efforts, the plea offer was reduced from 30 years to 19. The judge, in this case, was a tough judge who would sentence him to fifty years or more after trial.

After strongly urging the Defendant to plead guilty, and not take a hopeless case to trial, I was accused in open court by my client as being a sellout and working for the prosecution. In reality, by giving my client sound legal advice, that I was ethically and morally obligated to give, I was met with hostility and discharged. His new attorney took the case to trial, and to no one's surprise, other than the defendant's, there was a conviction. My former client lost the fight for his life. In all likelihood, he will die in jail before completing his 57-year sentence.

I once represented a man whose conviction for a double homicide was reversed and sent back for a new trial after he served ten years in jail. He was originally sentenced to fifty years to life. I was hired to conduct the second trial, which took place ten years after the initial conviction.

The case involved the robbery of a bar that served Friday fish fries, and was popular among factory workers who could cash their checks there on their payday. The robbery took place on payday because the bar had a lot of cash on the premises. Evidence in the first trial indicated that my client and two friends wore masks and were armed with gloves. They entered the bar and forced the patrons to lie on the floor. The owner was then forced to open the safe, and the money was removed. As the robbers were leaving, my client shot and killed two unarmed people for no apparent reason. The robbers divided the money, and hid the guns in the attic of my client's apartment, which he shared with his wife.

The original trial was reversed on appeal, because of prosecutorial misconduct. I filed a motion to dismiss the case before raising double jeopardy grounds. The United States Constitution provides that, in most circumstances, a person cannot be tried twice for the same argument. I provided the Court with legal authority, that when prosecutorial misconduct is intentional, double jeopardy attaches; and I requested a dismissal.

The judge ordered a hearing and directed the District Attorney, who tried to take the case, to stand and explain his misconduct. This presented a unique dilemma for the District attorney who was an elected official. If the District attorney testified that his misconduct was due to his own negligence, he would have made an embarrassing public admission that could lead to political consequences. If the district attorney testified that he understood the law, then his misconduct would have been ruled intentional, and a double murder case would have been dismissed.

After a lengthy hearing, the judge ruled that the prosecutor's misconduct was negligent, and ordered my client to stand trial. In between the hearing and trial, I received a plea offer that would have allowed my client's release from jail in two years; he had already been incarcerated for ten years. I suggested that he take the plea and run… remember, he was serving a fifty-year to life sentence.

Much to my surprise, my client refused the plea offer. He felt that he would have problems with the parole board, when released, and therefore, would likely end up back in jail. He explained to me that this was his second murder case. He had been out on parole for another murder when the double homicide occurred. He declined the plea offer and decided to go to trial.

When the trial commenced, the main evidence against him was his former wife's testimony that he had admitted the murder, the testimony of a jailhouse snitch concerning an alleged jailhouse confession, and a police testimony about recovering the guns from the attic. He was convicted, and is now serving out his fifty years to life sentence in a state prison.

In some ways, criminal defense lawyers are like doctors. Criminal defense attorneys solve client's legal problems; medical doctors solve patient's health problems. There are times you can go to a doctor and he can solve your problem with something as simple as an aspirin. Other times, your problem may be much more serious. The doctor may recommend the removal of a limb or organ, in order to save your life. The doctor who removes a limb or organ isn't a bad doctor because he couldn't save your life with an aspirin. Likewise, a lawyer in a hopeless case is not a bad lawyer for recommending a pea of guilty.

## Take Note!

Punishment, deterrence, rehabilitation and retribution are the main goals of the sentencing of a Defendant. After the verdict is reached, the judge will assign the term or severity of the sentence, which can be mandated as "with or without the chance of parole." Depending on the quality of time served, if parole is an option, the parole board will determine if the defendant has qualified to be released from prison before completing the full term of their prison sentence.

## Sentencing

Although the punishment should fit the crime, unfortunately, for countless African-Americans it does not. Sometimes the severity of the punishment is extremely unbalanced because of bias and racism in a particular jurisdiction. If the sentence is handed down as a result of a guilty verdict as opposed to a plea bargain, the judge will make a final decision after the trial is over depending on the evidence presented, the severity of the crime, the defendant's character and prior criminal history, and testimony from the victim as well as from the defendant's friends, family and associates. However, I'll give you a general assumption of how the system works or should work in conjunction with the various sentences mandated by the judge.

| | |
|---|---|
| **Execution** | The death penalty or capital punishment is being used in several states for the crime of murder. Unfortunately, until the courts find a foolproof way to absolutely prove the guilt of all defendants on death row, many innocent men and women are on death row waiting to be wrongfully executed. |
| **Life Sentence** | A life sentence is imposed on prisoners who are serious felons. They may have committed a third crime (under the 3 strikes law), performed an armed robbery , murder, or a violent sex crime. Generally, these crimes might merit a sentence of 25 years to life. |
| **Jail Term** | A convict can be sentenced for any term from as little as time served for a first-time felony up to a term for a more serious crime or concurrent terms that could add up to as many as fifty-five years. More often than not, parole could be recommended if the sentence is served without complication. Some states have adopted a "Boot Camp" program (referred to as "impact incarceration"), which could last up to six months for eligible offenders. |
| **Periodic Imprisonment** | This is a special program whereby offenders might spend one or more weekends a month in prison or a specific portion of their sentence. |

| | |
|---|---|
| **Probation** | This is an option that the judge can impose for a less serious crime; it does not involve imprisonment unless some of the terms of the probation are violated. |
| **Conditional Discharge** | This sentence is for minor offences for which a defendant might plead guilty. By participating in a court ordered supervised program, without committing another offense, the case against the defendant will be dismissed without a conviction. |
| **Restitution** | This is a court ordered payment to be made by the defendant to the victim, in the event that there were any financial losses suffered. It can be mandated in many states after a "guilty" verdict has been imposed. |
| **Fine** | The defendant may be ordered by the court (sometimes payable to a local charity) to pay a specific fee or fine as a stipulation of his or her probation. |

## Probation and Parole

Probation and parole are privileges and not rights. The privilege of being on probation or parole can be revoked if the rules and conditions set forth are not strictly complied with. If the probationer or parolee cannot follow the rules, he or she will simply be sent back to jail. The most common violation is continued drug or alcohol use.

Probation is an alternative to incarceration rather than sentencing a defendant to jail; a judge determines that the defendant is deserving of a break and sentences him or her to probation. The probationer must report to the probation office for a meeting on a weekly or biweekly basis, generally for three years if convicted of a misdemeanor and five years if convicted of a felony. (The length of time of probation may vary among jurisdictions).

Parole is an early release from prison. While on parole, the parolee is serving the balance of his/her sentence outside the prison. Sometimes before returning home, parolees are required to live in a halfway house. Parolees are required to report to their parole officer on a weekly or biweekly basis depending on their need for monitoring and supervision. Conditions are placed on parolees similar to those of probationers.

## FYI...Conditions

The judge places conditions on a defendant sentenced for probation. Typical conditions are as follows:

1. Report to the probation office as directed by the probation officer.

2. Submit to random drug testing.

3. Submit to random searches of your person, automobile, and home.

4. Undergo drug and alcohol counseling or other counseling directed by your probation officer.

5. Remain arrest free.

6. Report all contact with law enforcement.

7. Seek and maintain employment.

8. Attend school.

9. Refrain from consumption and use of alcohol.

10. Abide by a curfew set by the probation officer.

11. Do not associate with convicted felons.

12. Do not leave the state without permission from the judge.

I had a client named Albert, a promising basketball star who had been recruited by several major colleges. He smoked marijuana; and his drug use escalated to the point where he became a crack cocaine addict. He owed drug dealers a substantial amount of money. When they threatened his life for immediate payment, Albert went to a bank unarmed, handed the bank teller a note demanding money, and held his hand under his sweatshirt like he had a gun. The teller gave Albert money; he left the bank and gave the money to the drug dealers to pay his debt.

The FBI investigated the bank robbery. Albert was later arrested, based upon his picture recorded by the bank surveillance cameras. His mother was a nurse; his father was a business executive. Until they saw the surveillance photographs, both Albert's parents thought their son was wrongfully accused and that this was a case of mistaken identity.

Albert was eventually sentenced to four years incarceration in a federal prison. While in prison, he successfully completed numerous drug rehabilitation programs. When he was released from prison, he made contact with me and vowed that he would make a basketball comeback like Allen Iverson.

Albert's drug cravings got the best of him while he was on parole. When a urine sample came back testing positive for crack cocaine, Albert's parole officer understood his problem and enrolled him into a treatment program; but upon release from the drug program Albert continued using drugs. The parole officer had no other option than to file a violation petition and bring Albert back to court. The judge then sent Albert back to Federal Prison. *Unfortunately, Albert loved drugs more than his freedom.*

## An Appeal

The defendant has a right to appeal if he or she is found guilty after trial. Many times, when cases are plea-bargained the judge and prosecutor require the Defendant to waive his or her right to appeal as a condition of the plea.

## CRIME REPORT:
## "DEFENSE LAWYER WINS DISMISSAL FOR CLIENT FACING SERIOUS FELONY CHARGES"

One young African-American man was convicted and two others pleaded guilty to felony charges in connection to the sale of drugs. One of the three, however, had no criminal record and nothing to do with the big undercover drug deal that took place in the small town; his entire life could be ruined by these charges. As the brother of one and the cousin of the other accused drug dealer, he was an innocent young man who happened to be with them on the day they got arrested. All three young men faced substantial prison terms. As the defense attorney, my investigation proved that the former high school basketball star was not involved in the crime. Fortunately his case was dismissed.

## Always Remember...

My advice to probationers and parolees is that you must understand that parole and probation are privileges, and not rights.

▼ Do your best to establish a good relationship with your probation or parole officer. Keep away from other offenders. Those individuals will only get you into trouble.

▼ Stay away from drugs and alcohol. One marijuana cigarette or one hit on a crack pipe will give you a dirty urine sample and a direct ticket back to jail.

▼ Get a job. Improve your educational and vocational skills.

▼ Join a church and participate in church activities, including Bible Study.

▼ Stay away from the places that you once hung around; and do not associate with the same people you hung around with at the time you committed the crime, so that you don't get lured back into criminal activity.

*"An evil deed is not redeemed by an evil deed of retaliation.*
*Justice is never advanced in the taking of human life.*
*Morality is never upheld by legalized murder."*
—Coretta Scott King

## Chapter Eleven

# The Controversy Over Capital Punishment

## Know The Facts About The Death Penalty

The death sentence can be imposed upon you if you are convicted of a crime, such as *Murder for Hire, Witness Elimination* or *Serial Killing.* In addition, if a murder occurs during the commission of a crime associated with *Burglary, Arson, Kidnapping, Rape, Sodomy* or *Terrorism* that results in the death of one or more persons, you can also have a death sentence imposed on you if you receive a guilty verdict. However, unless, the jury vote is unanimous your life could be spared.

Whether someone is sentenced to life or death can depend more on his or her lawyer than on the crime. A defendant who cannot afford an experienced and competent lawyer is more likely to be sentenced to death than someone who can.

### Take Note!

Children have not reached a full understanding of their actions. However, in twenty-four states people can be sentenced to death for crimes committed when they were children.

The application of the death penalty is racist. Black and white people are the victims of violent crime in roughly equal numbers, yet 82 per cent of people executed since 1977 have been convicted of killing white victims. More than 350 people have been executed in the USA since 1990. More than 3,300 others are on death row.

In 1989 the US Supreme Court ruled that it was not unconstitutional to execute mentally retarded people, which resulted in approximately thirty mentally impaired people having been executed. Since then, approximately twelve states have adopted a law banning the execution of mentally retarded prisoners.

## Questionable Sentencing For Convicted Killers

Terry Nichols conspired with and assisted Timothy McVeigh in committing the Oklahoma City bombing. After a jury trial, Nichols, who is white, received a sentence of life without parole. McVeigh and Nichols together killed more fellow American citizens than any other Americans in our history.

Gary Leon Ridgeway, who is white, is better known as the Green River Killer. He recently pled guilty to forty-five counts of aggravated first-degree murder in a deal that gave him a sentence of life without parole. Ridgeway's sentence gave him more convictions than any other serial killer in United States History.

Should Nichols, McVeigh or Ridgeway have received the death penalty? Should Osama Bin Laden receive the death penalty, if captured and convicted of planning the September 11, 2001 hijackings and subsequent murders? Would you have a problem if the killers of Martin Luther King, Medgar Evers or Emmett Till received a death sentence? If you believe that the answer to any of these questions is "yes", then you believe in the death penalty.

## Jury Duty And Death Penalty Cases

People who do not believe in the death penalty are not eligible to serve as jurors in cases where death is a possible sentence. Because an overwhelming number of African-Americans who are called to jury duty claim to be against the death penalty, many African-Americans accused of capital crimes are tried before all-white juries.

When called to jury duty in a death eligible case, prospective jurors are questioned about their views about the death penalty by attorneys and by the judge involved in the case. Often, African-Americans called to jury duty have not fully examined their views on the death penalty. Most African-Americans are aware of the fact that, historically, the death penalty has been administered against African-Americans, and when questioned, tell the Court they are against it. By doing so, they have made a prosecutor's job easier because they have disqualified themselves from serving as a juror on the case.

In a death penalty case, the prosecutor's job is to get a conviction and convince a jury to kill the Defendant. It is easy for a prosecutor to get a conviction and death sentence if the jury is comprised of right-wing, law and order, pro-death penalty zealots.

There is a danger that innocent people will be convicted and sentenced to death because these pro-death penalty zealots are not going to critically challenge the prosecutor's case and the police investigation. The high legal standard of proof beyond a reasonable doubt is lowered. They are going to assume that the police arrested the right person without considering the possibility of mistaken identity, faulty scientific evidence, or lying informants. The death penalty zealots will listen to the testimony like a school of hungry sharks that smell blood in the water, and wait for the opportunity to vote for the execution of a human being.

## Take Note...

If capital punishment is going to be administered fairly, and in a color-blind way, there must be juries comprised of reasonable, fair-minded people. Potential jurors who have reservations about the death penalty can serve on juries if they are willing to consider death as an option in a death penalty case. There is no requirement for a juror to actually vote for death. In fact, it is illegal for a judge or prosecutor to require a juror to commit to a death sentence.

Death penalty trials have two phases. The first phase of a death penalty case is the guilt phase. If there is a finding of guilt after the first phase of the trial, then there is a second phase of the trial on the issue of sentencing. At this second phase, the jury will hear mitigating evidence about the Defendant concerning his or her life that helps the jury understand the person who committed the crime. Evidence of mental disorders, child abuse or neglect, unusual family circumstances, personal misfortunes and any other circumstances about the Defendant, that may convince a jury to spare the Defendant's life, is presented. The prosecutor will present aggravating factors, such as bad things about the Defendant or the crime in an effort to convince the jury to impose a sentence of death.

Jurors in death penalty cases are instructed that they "may" impose a death sentence if they believe the aggravating factors proved at trial, substantially outweigh mitigating evidence; and if so, they believe that death is the appropriate sentence. A juror is never required to vote for death. Twelve jurors must agree on a death sentence; if all twelve jurors cannot come to an agreement, then the judge will sentence the Defendant to life imprisonment.

It is important for each juror who serves on a death penalty case, to understand that if they vote for life, they do not have to explain their vote to anyone, including the judge, the prosecutor, the media, or even fellow jurors. A Defendant who is sentenced to life will receive a harsh sentence and spend the rest of his or her time in jail.

My message to African-Americans who are called to jury duty and have reservations about the death penalty is simple. You must be truthful when questioned by attorneys and the judge. Carefully examine your views about the death penalty before you go to court. Know that if you tell the judge and the attorneys that you are against the death penalty, you will be disqualified from jury service. Even if you have a problem with the administration of the death penalty in a discriminatory manner, you will have no vote on how it is applied in any individual case if you are disqualified from hearing the case.

If you believe that a death sentence was appropriate for Timothy McVeigh, and would be the proper punishment for Osama Bin Laden, or the murderers of Martin Luther King, Jr., Medgar Evers and Emmett Till, you are not anti-death penalty. If you truthfully tell the judge and the attorneys that you will listen to evidence and, if there is a conviction, you will consider death as an option for sentencing, you will not be disqualified from service. If you are selected as a juror, you will have the opportunity to save someone's life.

## FYI...Death Penalty Statistics

Since the reinstatement of the death penalty in the United States in 1976, there have been more than one hundred people convicted of capital crimes, sentenced to death, and later exonerated after spending on average more than eight years in prison. Of these, only twelve cases involved DNA evidence. During the same time period, 869 prisoners were executed. (Source: *American Friends Service Committee's Criminal Justice Program*).

## Living Or Dying...After A Death Sentence

Many convicted felons who live on "death row" have accepted their fate and do nothing but wait in silence. Many others become unruly, and even more dangerous to themselves and those living in prison with them. Many "convicted" felons, although they were found guilty and sentenced to die, are actually innocent of the crime for which they are being punished.

With the right support and extensive research, a handful of those men and women who have been wrongly convicted and sentenced to die manage to win their freedom. Exoneration, however, is not high on the list of "things to do" by public defenders, prosecutors or attorneys for hire; but it is becoming a priority by many organizations headed up by political and community activists.

When wrongfully-convicted murderer Ray Krone was exonerated by DNA evidence and released from Arizona State Prison in Yuma, he became the 100th death row exoneree. Sen. Patrick Leahy (D-VT) chief sponsor of the Innocence Protection Act (S.486), stated: "Our nation this week reached an infamous milestone: 100 known—and goodness only knows how many unknown—cases of people being sentenced to death, since the reinstatement of capital punishment, for crimes they did not commit. There should be no shame in errors made by well-meaning jurors, because human error is inevitable. But what is deeply shameful is a political and legal establishment that lives in denial. The time for denial is over. We know that the system has identifiable flaws. The system did not work for Ray Krone in his first trial, or in his second. We know that it has innocent victims. Ray Krone lost 10 years of his life while Arizona's women were endangered because the wrong man was in jail. We know the principal cause of its failings at the trial stage—incompetent and underfunded defense counsel—and we have a cheap and reliable post-trial tool at hand, DNA testing."

Many statewide programs have been formed to give support to wrongfully-convicted prisoners. For instance, more than 250 organizations in Pennsylvania have adopted moratorium resolutions in recent years, including the Pennsylvania Bar Association, the Pennsylvania Catholic Conference of Bishops, and the City Councils of Philadelphia, Pittsburgh, Erie, and six other municipalities.

In July 2003, Federal Court filing of DNA test results exonerating Nicholas Yarris, a Delaware County man on death row for twenty-one years, prompted renewed calls for a moratorium on executions and a thorough review of the Pennsylvania's death penalty system. The tests, conducted by Dr. Edward Blake, a nationally recognized expert in the field, excluded Yarris in the 1981 rape and murder of Linda Craig. This was the fifth exoneration of a death row prisoner since the Commonwealth reinstated capital punishment in 1978, and the first DNA exoneration based on DNA evidence. There are currently 239 people on Pennsylvania's death row, the fourth highest number in the U.S.

(Source: *American Friends Service Committee's Criminal Justice program*).

In 2002, Juan Melendez was released after serving more than 17 years on Florida's death row for a crime he did not commit. The prosecutor had lied to the jury, misleading them about the credibility of his witnesses in order to secure a conviction and death sentence. Melendez was the 24th prisoner to be exonerated and released from a death sentence in Florida since 1972. Florida leads the nation in wrongful convictions.

(Source: *Floridians for Alternatives to the Death Penalty*)

Unfortunately, when the wrongly convicted are exonerated and released back into society, they encounter further injustices and major obstacles. Many of those who were married have been divorced; and many of the family members and friends who supported them while on death row may have died or moved away.

Unlike parolees, exonerated prisoners are not entitled to social services, job training, placement or counseling to help them adjust to living in a dramatically different society than the one they left years earlier. In addition few states offer any financial compensation for their ordeal, and employers are wary of hiring them.

Only 16 states provide for the payment of reparations to innocent people convicted of crimes they did not commit and for which they are subsequently exonerated. Only New York and West Virginia have no limit. California caps reparations at $10,000, and the federal government is stingiest of all, granting a maximum of $5,000. The other 36 states provide no compensation at all.

(Source: *Truth in Justice Foundation*)

CRIME REPORT:
"ILLINOIS GOVERNOR IMPOSES
A MORATORIUM ON CAPITAL PUNISHMENT"

Of the more than 250 murder cases, in which a death sentence was imposed in Illinois courts between 1977 and 1999, twelve persons were executed, while thirteen persons were later released from prison because there was insufficient evidence that they were guilty. Most had established that they were not the perpetrators of the crimes for which they had been sentenced to die. Poor police work has been a major contributor to wrongful convictions and death sentences.

Illinois Governor George Ryan imposed a moratorium on further executions and in May 2000 he entered an Executive Order creating a Commission on Capital Punishment to study the capital punishment system in Illinois.

## Always Remember...

As a juror, you can make sure that an innocent person is not convicted of a crime. As a juror, you can overrule the overzealous, right-wing jurors if you vote for life because it takes twelve jurors in agreement for a death sentence.

*"Can't we all just get along?"*
—Rodney King

## Chapter Twelve
# Police Misconduct
# (Before, During & After Arrest)

### The Dangers of Racism in the Police Force

Throughout the U.S. African-Americans are being injured and even killed by police using excessive force or deliberately brutal treatment. Police have engaged in unjustified shootings, severe beatings, fatal chokings, and unnecessarily rough treatment. They are punching, kicking, beating, choking and shooting people who pose no threat, or are causing serious injuries, and sometimes death, by misusing restraints, chemical sprays or electro-shock weapons. Most reported incidents take place during arrest, searches, traffic stops or in street incidents.

One Christmas Day an unarmed African-American man, was shot dead in a New York supermarket by police who said they mistook the keys he was carrying for a gun.

Although the officer who shot him was cleared of wrongdoing, it was revealed that he had been involved in eight prior shootings. The New York Police Department (NYPD) Police Commissioner subsequently set up a monitoring system for officers involved in three or more shootings. (Source: *www.amnestyusa.com*)

Investigations into complaints of police brutality are often subject to delays and there are concerns about the quality and impartiality of internal investigations. Disciplinary action is rare. Sanctions, when they are imposed, are often lenient.

## Think About It!

*"A black teenager pedaling rapidly is fleeing crime. A white teenager pedaling at the same speed is feeling the freedom of youth."*

—National Association for the Advancement of Colored People commenting on the case of a black teenager shot by police after falling off his bicycle in Indianapolis, Indiana, March 1993

## The Other Face of Your Friendly Police Officer

While the proportion of repeatedly abusive officers on any force is generally small, responsible authorities—including law enforcement supervisors, as well as local and federal government leadership—often fail to act decisively to restrain or penalize such acts. Although, most police departments have strict guidelines on the use of deadly force, and international standards state that force should be used only as a last resort, proportionate to the threat and designed to minimize injury, it is clear that these standards are frequently breached and that too often the authorities have turned a blind eye to abuses.

Many police shootings raise serious doubts as to whether the victims posed an immediate threat. *Amnesty International* detailed more than 30 cases where NYPD officers had shot or injured suspects, including children, in disputed circumstances in its 1996 report. Nearly all the victims were black, Latino or from other minorities—a pattern seen across the country. Members of racial and ethnic minorities bear the brunt of police brutality in many areas. Black officers themselves have complained of the stereotyping of black men as criminal suspects.

An unarmed African-American woman, died after police from West Charlotte, North Carolina, fired 22 rounds at the car in which she was a passenger when it failed to stop at a police checkpoint. There was no evidence to suggest that anyone in the car was armed. Some police departments have introduced guidelines to bar police from firing at moving vehicles unless they are directly threatened with deadly force, but many have not. (Source: *www.amnestyusa.com*)

## Take Note!

The violations persist nationwide, in rural, suburban, and urban areas of the country, committed by various law enforcement personnel including local and state police, sheriff's departments, and federal agents. Every year there are thousands of reports of assault and ill-treatment by police officers.

## An Epidemic Of Cruelty Within The Prison System

As Attica Civil Rights Attorney, I heard first-hand information and saw the consequences of many severe injuries. My clients had suffered personally at the hands of certain prison guards and, after many years of trials and appeals they were compensated by the state for their losses.

Inmates across the country, including mentally ill prisoners, are being restrained in ways that are cruel, inhuman and sometimes life threatening. Restraint chairs—specially designed chairs that allow inmates to be immobilized—are widely used in prisons and jails despite the known dangers. One prisoner died of asphyxia when he was placed in a restraint chair with a towel wrapped over his face; it was later revealed that the jail system's 16 chairs had been used 600 times in six months.

Chemical sprays and electro-shock devices are also used; some have been banned because of the risks they pose. There is particular concern over the increasing use of remote control electro-shock stun-belts that, at the push of a button, inflict a powerful electric current causing severe pain and knocking the prisoner to the ground.

"Supermax" units are designed for long-term isolation of dangerous or disruptive prisoners; conditions in some constitute cruel, inhuman or degrading treatment or punishment. Prisoners are isolated in windowless concrete cells for 23 hours or more a day. They have no natural light and the solid steel doors have narrow slits, which allow only a minimal view of the corridor outside.

There have been numerous deaths in custody after police used restraint procedures known to be dangerous. Hogtying—tying suspects' ankles to their wrists behind their backs—has been recognized as highly dangerous for at least the past decade. However, while many departments, including the NYPD, have banned the procedure, others continue to use it. Deaths in custody resulting from hogtying have been reported from various parts of the country, including Athens (Georgia), Jackson (Mississippi), Memphis (Tennessee) and Washington, D.C.

## Police Abuse to Women in Prison

There is also a high rate of police abuse to women in prison, which directly conflicts with the internationally guaranteed human rights of women incarcerated in the United States. The types of abuse include: rape and other sexual assault by prison officials; shackling of pregnant prisoners, especially during labor, delivery and post-partum; seriously inadequate medical care leading to death, permanent injury, miscarriages and confinement in isolation for prolonged periods.

Health care in many facilities is seriously inadequate. Complaints include grossly deficient treatment for the mentally ill; lack of provision for women's health needs; failing to deliver prescribed drugs; and refusing or delaying necessary medical treatment.

Recently, a young pregnant woman in jail pleaded in vain with staff for medical help when she began bleeding. She eventually fell unconscious and was finally rushed to hospital, where her baby died.

In some institutions, rape and sexual abuse have persisted because inmates fear retaliation and feel too vulnerable to complain. Also of concern is the fact that staff of the opposite sex is allowed to undertake searches involving body contact and to be present where inmates are naked.

One situation involved an African-American woman, who was halfway through a 33-month sentence for credit card fraud at a Federal Correctional Institution. While the European American women were returned to the women's facility, she and the other African-American women were kept in the men's SHU. She complained when the prison authorities put her and several other women in the men's "Secure Housing Unit" (SHU); but nothing happened to help her. She complained that she was visible to male inmates and guards 24 hours a day, including when using the toilet and when she was in the shower; still nothing happened. She complained that she was taunted because she was a lesbian: "Maybe we can change your mind." She fought off one attacker in her cell with a broomstick; still, the prison officials did nothing. She gave a sworn affidavit to the authorities naming a guard who sold entry to her cell to male inmates as well as one of her attackers; still, nothing was done to protect her.

Late one night, three male inmates unlocked the door to the woman's cell. She was handcuffed, and then raped and sodomized, suffering severe injuries to her neck, arms, back, vaginal and anal areas. Her attackers called her a "snitch", told her to "keep her mouth shut", and threatened her with continued attacks if she kept complaining. In this case, the police didn't physically attack the woman; but their misconduct allowed her to suffer serious abuse while in their custody.

## FYI...
## Police Abuse is a National Concern

Inquiries into some of the largest urban police departments have uncovered systematic brutality.

Although police misconduct has been documented in fourteen cities, including: Atlanta, Boston, Chicago, Detroit, Indianapolis, Los Angeles, Minneapolis, New Orleans, New York, Philadelphia, Portland, Providence, San Francisco, and Washington, D.C., it is difficult to assess the true extent of police brutality because there is no reliable national data.

Since 1994, however, the federal government has been legally required to collect national data on police excessive use of force, but Congress has failed to provide the necessary funding.

## What You Can Do to Fight Police Misconduct:

The Human Rights Watch has provided the following suggestions:

▼ Write to your city government and urge that full funding be provided for citizen review of police officers accused of human rights violations.

   If your city, county, or town does not have citizen review of your police, call for the creation of an effective civilian review unit.

▼ Write to your city government and urge it to require your police department to create and utilize "early warning" or "at-risk" systems to identify officers who are the subjects of repeated complaints or civil lawsuits alleging misconduct.

   A small percentage of officers often taint an entire police force because police superiors do not act to hold them accountable by supervising, disciplining, or dismissing them when appropriate. An effective early warning system could make a difference.

▼ Write to your state legislators and governor urging them to create a special prosecutor's office to handle the investigation and prosecution of police officers accused of brutality or corruption.

Local prosecutors are often reluctant to pursue cases against officers they typically work with, and federal prosecutors are under-staffed and similarly reluctant.

Special prosecutors' offices in each state could go a long way toward prosecuting officers who commit criminal offenses; in turn, effective prosecution should act as a deterrent for officers who now believe they can avoid criminal prosecution for brutality in most cases.

CRIME REPORT:
"TWO YOUNG AFRICAN-AMERICANS ARE
FATALLY SHOT BY POLICE"

In separate incidents, two young African-Americans were fatally shot by the police. A 19-year-old passenger in a car pulled over by Chicago police after a short chase, was shot dead when officers mistook the cell-phone in her hand for a gun. Three months later, the Chicago Police Board (a police adjudicatory body) opened a hearing to decide on a recommendation by the police chief that the officers should be dismissed from the force. A day after the young woman was killed, Chicago police officers shot dead a former college football player, after he refused to get out of his car after a pursuit. He was shot when an officer smashed the car window and pointed his gun directly into the car. Both victims were black.

(Source: www.amnestyusa.com)

## Always Remember...

Don't hesitate to contact your local NAACP. They can document the details of the incident and help you by providing resources that would be beneficial to your case.

*"The only justification for ever looking down on someone is to pick them up."*
—Jesse Jackson

## Chapter Thirteen

# Casualties Of The War On Drugs

## Nobody Wins This War

There are no winners for those who are trying to win the drug game. I have been involved in the Criminal Justice System since 1979. As a New York State Trooper, I have arrested drug dealers. As an assistant district Attorney in Manhattan, I have prosecuted drug dealers. As a defense attorney in Buffalo, New York, I have defended drug dealers.

### Think Before You Act!

The story always has a bad ending; drug dealers either end up in jail or dead. With a little luck and a good defense attorney, sometimes a drug dealer can beat a few cases; but eventually he (or she) will get caught up in a sale or on a wiretap…and, it's off to jail.

On the streets, a drug dealer may duck a few bullets, and with the right kind of muscle, hold on to his territory for a little while, but eventually a fatal bullet will find him and he will lose the fight for his life.

The public perception of the life of a drug dealer is easy, fast money, women and good times. In real life, the opposite is true. Dealing drugs is probably the hardest job in the world; drug dealers are on duty 24 hours a day…that's why they carry cell phones and pagers.

117

They look out for police 24 hours a day; they get calls from their customers 24 hours a day; and, they have to look for rival drug dealers trying to rob them, kidnap them, or kill them all of the time.

It seems like drug dealers make a lot of money, but when you look at the fact that they are on duty 24 hours a day, what is their hourly wage? When they get raided, the police, who are searching for drugs, bust up their apartments and furniture. When drug dealers are arrested, they spend excessive amounts of money on expensive lawyers and bail bondsmen. While they are locked up, usually their friends and family steal any money that they have hidden away as stash; and the police will often seize their available money, their homes and cars because of asset forfeiture laws.

When drug dealers are in jail, they are not really making any money. If you consider the time that they spend in jail as time on the job, they probably make less than minimum wage. For instance, if a drug dealer earns $100,000.00 in one year and in the next year, after being caught, he is sentenced to twenty years in jail, he will be reduced to earning less than $5,000 a year. To make matters worse, while in jail, the drug dealer will still be working seven days a week, 24 hours a day.

I once represented a tough guy named Bone, who moved to Buffalo from Chicago. He claimed that, while in Chicago, he was a member of the Gangster Disciples gang. Bone moved into a large, low-income housing complex in Buffalo. He was arrested several times for narcotics activity; but, due to incompetent police work, I was able to get those charges dismissed.

Bone also had a reputation as someone who would hurt anyone who would mess with him on his drug territory; rumor had it that he would shoot people, but not kill them. Bone wanted the people he shot to be a "living" example that he was not to be messed with. Eventually Bone got caught with a gun; and he was convicted. After the trial, Bone was sent to prison for seven years. A couple of years into his prison sentence, I received a call from his relatives and a pastor; Bone had contracted a terminal disease while in jail; I suspect that the disease was AIDS. I was asked to assist Bone in getting an emergency release from jail to parole. Four weeks later Bone lost the fight for his life; he died in a prison hospital.

I once defended a sixteen-year-old drug dealer named Richie; he had a baby-face and a stone-cold heart. Richie was convicted of manslaughter for shooting his friend between the eyes. In his confession to the police, Richie explained that he and his friend were fighting over ten dollars of drug money. He told police that when he pointed the gun at his friend, he heard that friend say, "I don't mind dying." Richie responded, "I don't mind killing you either," and pulled the trigger.

In the early 1990's, Tommy, who was an eighteen-year-old marijuana dealer, attended a church where I was going at the time. He was having problems with some "Jheri Curl" brothers in their 30's, who also sold marijuana. Tommy was arrested after he sprayed the "Jheri Curl" brothers' house with bullets. When he went to court, I talked to the "Jheri Curl" brothers and Tommy about having a truce. I told them that there was no need to keep trying to kill each other. They all shook hands and agreed to end their beef. The "Jheri Curl" brothers never came to court again; and the charges against Tommy were dismissed.

I had a chance to talk to Tommy about getting out of the drug game and he agreed that it was about time. However, his girlfriend had just had a baby and he had to stay in the game a little longer, in order to pay child support.

I learned later that Tommy and the "Jheri Curl" brothers did more than end their beef; they became partners in crime and combined their marijuana distribution business. One day, as I watched the early morning news, I learned that Tommy was murdered in a drug house. He had been hit by a shotgun blast fired through the window.

I attended Tommy's funeral, and afterwards, one of the "Jheri Curl" brothers told me he wanted to hire me; he explained that he had applied for a pistol permit and needed legal representation. I declined to accept the case.

## Racial Profiling and How It Affects the Victims of the War On Drugs

Although government surveys reveal that African-Americans constitute only thirteen percent of drug users, the arrest rates for drug offenses continue to rise at an alarming proportion. This includes drug possession, as well as drug trafficking, both of which can lead to conviction and incarceration.

### Take Note!

Racial profiling contributes heavily to the African-American arrest rate, as the criminal justice system determines which neighborhoods to patrol, when and where to make drug arrests and the imminent mandatory sentencing.

The War on Drugs, which began in the early 1980's, resulted from the demands of politicians to get tough on drug offenders. The ensuing pressure forced the police department to literally "declare war"; and their simple logic directed them to focus on African-Americans in hopes to increase the probability of seizing contraband. "Racial profiling" on the streets and highways has become a major vehicle in finding drug offenders who are just driving in the wrong place at the wrong time. Are police singling out African-Americans for minor traffic infractions, hoping to be able to charge them with something more significant?

Unknown to many officers, "Driving while Black" is not a crime; but if you resist arrest, it can lead to physical harm or even death. (How many innocent people died as a result of Rodney King's DWB). Of course, if you do commit a "major" traffic violation, you can legally be stopped...and arrested...and have your vehicle seized. (Now, you're "in the criminal justice system".) The fact is that just one out of thirty cars pulled over may produce drugs; and sometimes this might be only a single "joint". Too often, these illegal searches have caused great distress to the alleged drug offender who couldn't afford legal representation; planted evidence has contributed heavily to the African-American prison population.

In an attempt to curtail drug trafficking, the War on Drugs has extended beyond the communities into very public places. Several thousands of African-American travelers in bus terminals, railroad stations and airports have been victims of "racial profiling". Police or even federal agents have approached African-American men, women and teens; and they have been searched and temporarily relieved of their luggage, just because they "fit the profile". Some of the accused may just be black, short, tall, well-dressed, not so well-dressed, wearing dreads, braids or a head wrap, carrying a brief case or back-pack; they may have purchased their ticket with cash an hour before their scheduled departure; or, they may have missed their connection while their luggage proceeded to their final destination ahead of them.

## Drug Crimes Have Affected Generations of African-Americans

Drug crimes have removed more African-Americans from their homes than any other types of crimes. In addition to the financial and emotional hardships caused to families of the drug offenders, our communities and the nation stand to suffer serious consequences. Because state policies disenfranchise current or ex-felons, about one in seven African-Americans of voting age, cannot vote. Thus, those persons who are most likely to maintain unfair policies may remain in or be elected to political office by an indifferent population.

Unfortunately, in many communities, it is more likely to find discrepancies in the sentencing of African-Americans for less serious drug-related offenses. The differences lie in whether a drug user or drug trafficker will get sentenced to parole, minimal jail time, or (under the three strikes law) up to life in prison; and if the crime involves murder, the sentence can even result in the death penalty.

When the accused is African-American, the scales of justice have already been tipped and the punishment promises to be more severe. The "War on Drugs" has proven to be the most significant factor leading to the increasing population of African-Americans in prison. Most prominent in the racial disparity is the difference in sentencing for crack cocaine versus powder cocaine.

At the federal level, whether you are in possession of **five hundred grams** of **cocaine powder** or only **five grams** of **crack cocaine**, the sentence results in a "mandatory" five years in prison. Studies show that African-Americans comprise almost 90 percent of the defendants charged with crack cocaine offenses. During the last several years, those percentages represent hundreds of thousands of new inmates and have resulted in hundreds of new prisons being built around the country.

Think about it! A big time drug dealer may be caught with up to 499 grams of cocaine powder; if its his first offense, he could feasibly beat the mandatory five year sentence and receive a one-year prison term. Now, that same cocaine powder could be refined and sold in the community to an addict or a dealer in five-gram packages. Guess what! That can earn you a five-year mandatory prison term!

So, as the African-American population gets picked up and locked up, little by little, our political rights diminish. Those persons who have less going for them—declining employment, housing and educational opportunities—inevitably have become "targets" of the War on Drugs. Because many African-Americans have lost their right to vote, we have less say in what happens in the local, state and national governments. The vicious cycle of depression and poverty continues; and we lose far more than we'll ever gain for our families, our children and ourselves.

## Facts About the Costs of Being Involved In the War on Drugs
(Source: *Drug Clock*—www.drugsense.org)

▼ Every twenty seconds, someone is arrested for a drug law violation.

▼ In the year 2000, 646,042 people were arrested for drug possession, which was 46.5 percent of the total 1.5 million drug arrests that year.

▼ In 2003, there were more than 1.6 million arrests for drug law violations.

▼ During the year 2003, nearly 250,000 people were incarcerated for drug law violations.

▼ In 2003, the U.S. federal government spent over 19.2 billion dollars at a rate of about $609 per second on the War on Drugs; state and local governments spent at least another 20 billion dollars.

CRIME REPORT:
"SMALL TOWN SERVES UP STIFF JAIL SENTENCES IN AN EFFORT TO WAGE WAR ON DRUG CRIMES."

A small town in the state of New York, with a population of under 50,000 is one of several towns that have cracked down on drug crime. To discourage alleged drug dealers from fleeing big cities in order to set up shop in one particular small town, the police chief "strongly advised" landlords to evict their tenants who were known to be involved in illegal drug activities. He also beefed up the arrest rates for drug users and drug traffickers and mandated stiffer sentencing policies.

After being dragged from under his bed, a twenty-year old slaying suspect was arrested, charged with first-degree murder for killing a man during a burglary-attempt. My client and two other young men had entered the victim's apartment to look for marijuana that they thought he was selling. They didn't find any marijuana, but were believed to have stolen other property after the victim was killed. *Although only one young man actually pulled the trigger, all three were charged with first-degree murder, first-degree robbery and first-degree burglary.*

## Always Remember...

Whether they are using or selling crack cocaine, African-Americans are punished far more severely for a seemingly far less offense.

*"Children have never been very good at
listening to their elders, but they have
never failed to imitate them."*
—James Baldwin

## Chapter Fourteen
# Women In Prison—The Endless Cycle of Punishment

During the last twenty years the incarceration rate for women has increased from 12,300 to more than 150,000; in just 5 years, from 1986 to 1991, the number of African-American female drug offenders in state prison rose by 828%. During the period of 1986 to 1995, 91% of female drug offenders entering the criminal justice system in New York were members of racial and ethnic minorities; by 1995 one in every seven women arrested for a drug offense was sentenced to prison. African-American women accounted for 47% of those women.

Women are predominantly arrested for non-violent offenses, many of them drug-related. Usually when a woman commits a violent offense, it is most likely against someone close to her.

### Take Note!

The common thread between the women inmates is that many are low income, uneducated, substance abusers and suffering from some degree of mental illness. Many of them have been physically or sexually abused; one-third of the women in prison have been raped.

Two-thirds of the women in prison are the heads of their household and have children under eighteen. While many of them already experiencing parenting problems, due to their involvement in drugs or crime, being locked-up just makes it worse for their children. Half of the women incarcerated don't see their children at all during their prison terms; many of them are raised in foster care.

Some prison systems are attempting to raise the level of interaction between mothers and their children, by encouraging children's visitation, offering parenting classes and allowing women with babies to have their children live with them in prison for a period of time. This is a good thing for those women who are genuinely sorry for committing their offense.

Three-quarters of the women arrested for drug possession have no prior criminal record. Many of them appear in court, without an attorney and plead guilty to a minor felony charge; they may get probation or a few months in jail. Now, they're in the system. Upon their release, many women get no substance-abuse treatment and drift back to their old habits.

Even though they may be low-level offenders with minor criminal histories, because of their drug addiction, many African-American women come back as second felony offenders and receive lengthy, mandatory prison terms.

In addition to time served, in some states, the severity of a woman's punishment associated with her drug addiction can be extremely harsh. She may be banned for life from receiving welfare benefits; she may lose access to student loans for higher education; she may be banned from living in Public Housing; and she may lose her right to vote. Depending on the impact of the punishment placed on the woman and her children, these factors can lend to the deterioration of that woman's community.

The well-being of children is intimately linked to the well-being of their parents. Children who are neglected are almost as likely victims of physical abuse to engage in violent crimes during adolescence and adulthood.

Temporary Assistance for Needy Families (TANF) is a federal block grant program that imposes time limits and work requirements on welfare recipients. However, nearly 50,000 African-American women who would ordinarily be eligible have been banned for life or partially banned from receiving cash assistance and food stamps. This is part of a ruling in 42 participating states that prevents convicted drug offenders from receiving welfare benefits. (Ironically, murderers and other felons are not affected by this ruling). (Source: *The Champion: Food Stamps & The Criminal Justice System*)

Fortunately, the benefits to the children will still be intact, but without the mother's stipend, an already diminutive budget becomes even less. Needless to say, due to the prospect of reduced family income, hundreds of thousands of African-American children, who are at risk of neglect and malnutrition, are suffering because of this ban. To make matters work, there is a growing shortage of drug treatment programs which makes it more difficult for drug addicts to get treatment and therefore lead a more fruitful life; and those programs that are available recommend that female offenders focus on their recovery for the first six months instead of getting a job.

In order to "make it" from prison or probation to the community, women would need sufficient resources and/or social networks; but let's face it, these are uncommon links in the African-American community. According to the Department of Justice, *"nearly 30% of the women in prison are on welfare at the time of their arrest."* Where will these women turn to for help, as if trying to kick the habit isn't stressful enough? In addition to all the other problems that occur, homelessness is on the rise. How can they manage and where will they live after prison?

Unfortunately for too many, there's the revolving door syndrome. Many of the women can't make the transition; they find themselves back on drugs and perhaps even selling them, or selling their bodies to buy them, or stealing. A growing number are losing their children to the child welfare system, to the streets, or because of neglect or intentional abuse to death. (Source: *The Department of Justice*)

## Take Note!

According to the Philadelphia Department of Human Services, "*If a mother is not able to support her child, we would take the child; and at the end of twelve months of placement, we have to terminate parental rights unless there are compelling circumstances. If you've made a mistake in your life, it's very punitive…as more and more women lose their benefits…women will lose their kids, will lose everything in their lives—cash assistance, kids, jobs. Employers won't hire them with a felony drug conviction.*"

(Source: *Philadelphia Department of Human Services*)

Women sentenced to probation, even though they may have a felony conviction tend to do better in the job market; almost half of the African-American women in prison were unemployed at the time of their arrest. Many without jobs have young children and are receiving welfare benefits.

More than 40% of African-American women on probation or in prison have not completed high school; these statistics mixed with a criminal record do not spell success on the job market. A key factor contributing to low wages, underemployment and unemployment is the lack of a formal education. Many correctional institutions offer general education programs, but for the most part, the acquired skills are inadequate for landing a meaningful job upon release.

The vocational training offered to women in prison is geared to keep them in low-income positions, such as: clerical work, telemarketing, cleaning, kitchen work and sewing. *(How does a woman support a family with an $8 an hour job?)*. Although there are some job training programs offered to ex-offenders, for those with drug convictions, federal aid may be either denied or delayed for a two-year period.

Some states have banned ex-offenders from obtaining college financial aid, public employment and occupational or professional licenses in fields such as: childcare, social work, health care and accounting. It's up to these women to seek the help they need; but they must first find the inner piece and belief in themselves that will help them know that what they do matters to those who love them.

Trying to get back on track, as an ex-offender and drug abuser will be extremely difficult. These women should be given the time and assistance needed to build marketable skills, which will probably require further training in the areas where they know they won't be excluded from the job market. Upon their release from prison, if information is not offered to them, they should ask for it. Transitional assistance is always available.

Don't fall back into a trap. Many African-American women were led into the criminal arena by their male counterparts. For some, the children came first, then the abuse, then the drugs, then the crime. It could have been in a different order, but usually there was pain involved and the need to escape it; drugs probably seemed like the only escape. Once these women stepped aboard, it became a vicious cycle; half of the women in prison were using drugs at the time of their offense and most of them committed the offense to support their drug habit.

## Think Before You Act!!

For low-income women, in particular, crack-cocaine was, and is, their greatest source of addiction. Besides affecting the mind, crack-cocaine increases a woman's exposure to violence and abuse; and often leads her into prostitution. By 1997, one in every five female inmates in New York state prisons was HIV positive.

For most African-American women who are substance-abusers, if they have remained outside the criminal justice system and decided to seek help, there is no affordable outpatient treatment; their low-income jobs do not afford them the benefit of health insurance. For many of those women, because they couldn't get help, their drug habit got worse and they ended up on the wrong side of the law. Once they are released from prison, they will qualify for free drug treatment; but for many, it may be too late to fully recover. Residential drug treatment programs are probably the best chance a woman has upon her release from prison. Some programs offer a place for the woman to live with her children for a specified time; other programs will force a woman to choose between treatment and her children because of inadequate facilities; and some programs may just be out of space.

Until funding for drug prevention and treatment has increased enough to serve those in need of it, the incarceration rate of drug abusers will continue to rise. For instance, in 1998 five million people were in need of drug treatment, but only two million received it. One-third of the federal drug budget is used for prevention and treatment, while two-thirds is used for law enforcement and incarceration.

With an adequate support system, many African-American women could overcome their drug addiction and avoid the criminal justice system, making the difference in their lives, in their children's lives and in their communities.

## FYI...Facts:

▼ Approximately 148,000 women are incarcerated in US jails and prisons.

▼ The number of US women inmates has more than tripled since 1985.

▼ About 40% of women in prison violated drug laws. About 25% are in prison for committing a violent crime.

▼ Black women's rate of imprisonment is more than 8 times that of white women.

▼ Hispanic women's rate of imprisonment is nearly 4 times that of white women.

▼ Around 200,000 children under the age of 18 have an incarcerated mother.

▼ 80,000 women in US prisons and jails are parents; many are single parents.

▼ 1,300 babies were born to women in prison in 1997-98 and more than 2,200 pregnant women were incarcerated.

*(Sources: The Crisis Magazine, "The Color Line/Some Punishments Begin After Prison; The Sentencing Project" (November 1999), "Gender and Justice—Women, Drugs, and Sentencing Policy and The Sentencing Project" (February 2002). "Life Sentences—Denying Welfare Benefits to Women Convicted of Drug Offences)*

## CRIME REPORT:
## "WOMAN GUILTY IN BOYFRIEND'S FATAL STABBING"

A judge found my client guilty of a lesser charge of first-degree manslaughter in the fatal stabbing of her boyfriend in a crack-house. The State Supreme Court Justice who conducted a two-week, non-jury trial found the 40-year-old woman innocent of two counts of second-degree murder. I told the judge that she was "a mentally disturbed person" and an example of how crack cocaine users run the risk of either being killed or killing somebody; she had a history of drug and alcohol abuse and manic depression.

The victim had been a US Postal mail handler; my client had been a state government secretary for eleven years. She told the judge that she killed her boyfriend after a week-long drug party, stabbing him in the chest, groin and above the eyes. The victim's brother in law testified that he had been trying to overcome his drug problem and that my client continued to pester him to buy more ….she had even pulled a gun on him once. She was ordered to serve 8 ½ to 25 years in prison.

## Always Remember...

Poverty caused by any means can be construed as a direct cause to the rise in crime in the African-American community. Mixed with drug intake, parental imprisonment and abuse it becomes a deadly cocktail, inherent for failure.

*"The only thing worse than failing is
being afraid to try. Wait means never!*
—Reverend Dr. Martin Luther King, Jr.

## Chapter Fifteen
# Facts and Advice for
# Victims of Domestic Violence

This is the only chapter of this book written for the protection of crime victims. African-American women are victims of domestic violence at an alarming rate. I have represented firefighters, attorneys, factory workers, bus drivers, drug dealers, police officers, insurance agents and people from all walks of life accused of domestic violence.

In each case, I have been involved in where there was real domestic violence, and not falsely reported violence; I have tried to protect the victim from future domestic violence. I have done my best to assure that my client's actions were not repeated, and that he received appropriate counseling. I have also advised my clients to refrain from any offensive conduct towards their partners.

I hope that my efforts have assisted victims of domestic violence with the fight for their life, while at the same time, protecting and vigorously defending the rights of my clients.

## FYI...Statistics

In the United States, almost 4.5 million women are injured by their partners or spouses each year, according to FBI Uniform Crime Statistics. One-third of female murder victims are killed by their spouse or partner. More than 53% of male abusers also abuse their children.

## The Three Stages Of Domestic Violence

According to the Domestic Abuse Intervention Project, domestic violence is a cycle. The three stages of domestic violence are:

1. Tension building
2. Acute explosion
3. "Honeymoon"

The tension building stage involves the batterer nitpicking and arguing. He will attempt to isolate his partner from family and friends. Passive aggression, such as withdrawal, is a symptom of this stage, along with drinking, destruction of property and criticism.

The acute explosion stage is the most dangerous in the cycle of violence. Symptoms of this stage include violent behavior, such as: hitting, choking, humiliation, imprisonment, verbal abuse and rape.

The third stage of the cycle of violence is the honeymoon. The batterer attempts to win back the affections of the victim. He will beg forgiveness, promise to change and get counseling, give flowers and other gifts, and enlist family support. Most often, the batterer will be given another chance, and the cycle will repeat again and again.

Women must understand that when police are called to investigate a claim of domestic violence, and there is proof that the crime occurred, the police must make an arrest. The offender will be taken away in handcuffs and kept in custody until a judge releases him. The judge can order the offender to be removed from the home; and he can issue an order of protection directing the offender to have no contact with his accuser.

Most prosecuting agencies have a "no-drop" policy. That means that the charges will not be dropped just because the victim decides she wants the charges dropped. Generally, the prosecutor will require extensive counseling in anger management before considering dropping the charges or allowing the defendant to plead guilty to reduced charges. In instances where the victim does not want to cooperate with authorities, they will be subpoenaed to court.

I have encountered situations where a court order required the man to live outside the house, and the woman wanted the man to come home. The court wouldn't allow the man to come home until he completed a lengthy intensive program. This caused a hardship on the family, both financially and emotionally. The children and wife all wanted the man to come home; the woman felt the courts had victimized her.

The wife of former NFL great Jim Brown is a woman who felt victimized by a prosecutor's office no-drop policy. In a television interview, Jim Brown's wife stated in substance that she called the police to quiet an argument; she did not want her husband sent to prison. Unfortunately, prosecutors subpoenaed Mrs. Brown to court and he was convicted of damaging her car; Jim Brown was eventually sentenced to six months in prison.

## Take Note!

My advice to women is to recognize the symptoms of domestic violence, and seek counseling at the tension building stage and before the acute explosion stage. If your partner will not cooperate, you can go to a family court and file a family offense petition. You will have a greater input into the resolution of a case in family court than in criminal court. Additionally, early intervention is more often successful than intervention at a later time. If your case is in a criminal court and you believe that you are treated unfairly, you may want to consult with or hire an attorney.

## Orders of Protection

One common mistake that couples involved in domestic violence cases make is violating orders of protection. When a judge issues an order of protection, only a judge can rescind or cancel the order. I have seen instances where an order of protection has been issued and the woman has invited the man to return home and he does so. The man has now committed the very serious crime of criminal contempt. An invitation by the victim to return home is no defense to violating an order of protection.

Unfortunately, many victims of domestic violence lose the fight for their lives, and end up murdered by their partners.

The Erie County District Attorney's Office advises victims of domestic violence who fear for their lives to have a personalized safety plan.

### Personalized Safety Plan

▼ Avoid staying alone. Have someone stay with you and escort you in and out of work, school, etc.

▼ Change your daily routine and the places you usually go.

▼ Change or add locks to your house so your partner does not have access.

▼ Talk with your neighbors, landlord, employer and friends about your situation so they can help look out for you.

▼ Make a list of people you trust to call in case of an emergency.

▼ Teach family, children and friends a "code word or sign" to let them know you need help.

▼ Teach children how to use the telephone to call the police.

▼ Plan safe places to retreat if an emergency occurs—avoid rooms with no exits (bathroom), or with potential weapons (kitchen).

▼ Save and document all contracts, messages or incidents with your partner. Keep a log with dates and times and what occurred.

▼ Screen phone calls, change your phone number or buy a caller ID.

▼ If you have to meet your partner, meet in a public place with someone you trust.

▼ Keep a list of important numbers for local shelters, DA's office, police, etc.

▼ Watch for clues or signs that your partner's anger may be escalating.

## If You Have an Order of Protection

▼ Call the police if your partner violates the order in any way; then call the District Attorney's office and notify them of the incident.

## Always Keep a Copy With You

▼ Make copies of your order of protection and give them to your local police station, employer, landlord, your children's school and daycare.

▼ If you lose your order, you can obtain a copy from the District Attorney's Office.

## Other Items to Keep Nearby

▼ Money, checkbook, credit cards

▼ Personal papers: Driver's license, Social Security Card, Welfare ID, Birth certificates, etc.

▼ Keys, medications

▼ Court papers, police reports

## CRIME REPORT:
## "WOMAN DIALED 911 IN FIGHT FOR HER
## LIFE...DIES AT THE HANDS OF THE POLICE"

When the 31-year old woman dialed 911 for help from the police, she never dreamed that they would be the ones responsible for her death. She had called twice because the police were slow to respond. There was a domestic dispute between the victim and her boyfriend; and in the process, he had punched her in the mouth.

By the time the officers arrived at my client's house, she was very upset and met them outside to see why it took them so long. The policeman who shot her in the chest with his 9mm pistol claimed she had charged at him with a butcher knife. Ten months later, my client died of organ failure complications.

## Always Remember...

Despite counseling, court orders and police intervention, the abuser will stalk, harass, threaten and eventually kill the woman who has spurned his affection.

*"There are two types of leaders: those who protest
and those who take action by building institutions"*
—Rev. Floyd Flake

## Chapter Sixteen
# Cutting Down on Crime in Your Community

### Rebuilding Our Communities

We must seek to restore the communities that have been simultaneously ravaged by crime and the criminal justice system. To accomplish this, we must reinforce and support community organizations in the inner cities, as well as change the way we respond to crime itself. This can be done by adopting a more effective approach to criminal punishment and by rebuilding our communities.

I mentor teenagers, and share my successes with them; it is so rewarding when I know I have reached them. I always urge young people not to take the easy way out; and let them know that if someone tells them they can make a lot of money selling drugs, "don't do it!" It's not worth it.

One of the biggest challenges I have is teaching young people patience…they want everything now. Success takes a long time and you have to start at the bottom. I worked seven days a week and had a second job at night to put myself through college; working every day for four years was very hard. Life didn't get any easier when I graduated from college. Here I was with a college degree; the first and only job I could find was a city job—collecting garbage. To make it worse, during my interim as a garbage collector, the circus was in town and with the circus, came the elephants. Guess who had to shovel up those huge piles of manure? Now, that's what I call starting at the bottom.

## Looking For The Happy Endings

There are so many stories to tell; some have happy endings; many don't. Unfortunately, for those that don't, it's because the children had no mentors, no role models, no one to guide them through life. So many African-American families have been affected by the incarceration of a family member; and too often it's the head of the household. So many African-American children have been victims of abuse and poverty; and for them comes the vicious cycle that repeats the hardships in the households that they now head up as adults. Sometimes, but not often enough, community people and organizations will dedicate a part of their life to those young people who live in pain.

> ## Take Note!
> For decades, we have relied on mass incarceration—a policy that has robbed inner city communities of whole generations of African-American men. We respond to crime in a self-defeating way, by stigmatizing criminals and cutting them off from their families and their community; thus, we encourage further criminal behavior and undermine one of the most important deterrents to crime: a sense of belonging.

At a recent community event, a prominent African-American businessman shared his painful childhood story with the audience. His mother was a domestic and his father was a war veteran, who had to work in menial jobs. Like so many other Black men, the boy's father had been beat down by the system. He took his anger and frustration out on his wife and son by inflicting painful beatings on them.

As early as 6 years old, the boy could remember thinking that he had to get out of the house. He lived in a multi-cultural community, with a nice Italian neighborhood grocer. One day, as the boy and his friends were preparing to steal some ice cream from a truck, the grocer grabbed him by the ear and took him aside. He told the boy that he knew his family and they were good people; he also let the boy know, in no uncertain terms, that he shouldn't steal, and that he would embarrass his family by getting into trouble. Then the grocer instructed him to report to work the next morning. The boy had his first job taking out the fruit baskets, sorting the fruit, and helping to make and deliver sandwiches to the Italian construction workers.

The grocer had taught the boy about honesty and integrity and instilled in him some valuable work ethics that would stay with him throughout his life. He learned things like how to look people straight in the eyes, without staring because you can tell a lot about a person by their eyes and their body language. The grocer also taught him to listen to what people said, but hear what they meant. The boy never forgot the grocer's advice; and has grown into a well-respected man who has changed thousands of lives through his work, deeds and community outreach.

## Organizing To Re-Build Your Community

Around the country, many concerned citizens, with similar stories, have formed organizations to help families who have become victims of our society. They organize community clean-up campaigns so that the inner-city residents can feel better about where they live; they help the parents further their education, find jobs, get housing and food; they try to discourage drug dealers from infiltrating their communities and talk to gang members about doing good things with their manpower; they sponsor sports leagues and coach the players; they organize rap sessions between the elderly and the youth so that they learn to respect one another; they help the high school students find scholarships for college.

One of the biggest problems that the community organizations have had to address is illiteracy; it is a very common among inmates. One-half of all adults in federal and state correctional institutions cannot read or write at all and, only about two-thirds of those in prison have not completed high school. The lack of education leads to the lack of opportunities; and the lack of opportunities leads to more crime.

Unfortunately, the many budget cuts have greatly affected community programs; many have closed; and many of those programs still in existence have to rely on private funding or the generosity of volunteerism. Because of the lack of funding, a growing number of our elected officials have turned a deaf ear on the problems plaguing the inner cities, and become ineffective in the fight for our lives.

Double standards in the criminal justice system have also had a devastating impact on African-American communities. The racial divide fostered by inequality in criminal justice has contributed to both the rise in crime and the decay of the inner city—factors that wear away the sense of community that encourages conformity with the criminal law.

We must make a great effort to vote for those politicians who are concerned about our well-being. Only then, will our communities become safe, prosperous and revitalized.

## CRIME REPORT: "ATTORNEY ADVISES TEENS ON STAYING OUT OF TROUBLE"

Taking time out from my law practice to mentor inner-city teenagers has always been important to me. I want them to learn about the ins and outs of the criminal justice system and offer them my support as knowledge about growing up in the inner-city. I had a great role model when I was growing up—my late father (who was the city of Olean's first firefighter) and my first basketball coach.

I always tell young people "If you want to stay out of trouble, surround yourself with good people and emulate those who set a good example…someone like your father who works hard and brings home the money…someone like your coach who teaches you about being a team player and playing fair."

## Always Remember…

Until we all begin to see the problem of inequality in criminal justice as our own, and take responsible measures to respond to it, our crime problem and racial divide will only get worse.

*"Father only means that you are taking care of your children. That's what it means to be a father. It doesn't mean having babies. Anybody can make a baby, but a father helps to raise his children. There is another word for fatherhood. It's called responsibility"*
—Malcolm X

## Conclusion
# Reshaping Our Youth

Yes, there is discrimination in our Criminal Justice System. However, eliminating discrimination in the system alone will not solve the problem of the high incarceration rate of African-Americans. I believe that reshaping the attitudes of our youth and our community will do the most good.

For instance, in my law practice, I often come across young African-American females living at home, who are involved with drug dealers. Their mothers allow the relationship to continue because drug dealers are buying their daughters clothes and jewelry and giving them money. I have often spoken to young girls in that situation, and asked them why they don't get a guy who is in school and working a part-time job. The typical response is "The drug dealer can do more for me. I like my men hard." Apparently, the guy in school is too much of a nerd.

The end result is the young girl gets pregnant and drops out of school. The drug dealer gets arrested and sent to jail for a long time, or is murdered. The child of the teenager is then raised by an unfit mother or grandmother receiving welfare; and the cycle continues.

I have represented too many African-American teenagers who sell drugs. The drug dealing is tolerated by their mothers because they are helping mom pay the bills. In actuality, the mothers are co-conspirators and beneficiaries of their son's or daughter's drug dealing activities. When their sons and daughters get murdered or sent to jail, the mothers blame the system.

I recently represented "Larry", who was arrested for drug possession. Larry's mother was furious because when the police arrested him, he was punched in the face, and had a black eye. Larry's mother seemed to be more angry at the police officer, who punched and arrested her son than she was at her son, who had crack cocaine in his possession. She wanted to sue the police officer.

"Larry" was a first-semester college student. I told him and his mother that I was the wrong attorney to hire if they wanted to sue the police officer who punched "Larry". I gave them a dose of reality when I said that juries do not award crack dealers money when police officers punch crack dealers in the eye during the course of an arrest. I said that jurors would probably congratulate and shake the hand of the officer who arrested and punched "Larry". I then asked "Larry" why he had the drugs. He said he was selling drugs to pay bills and to help his mom out. I asked "Larry" why he wasn't working, and he told me he didn't have time to work because he was playing basketball and wanted to make the college basketball team.

I told "Larry" and his mother that if he wanted me to take the case, he would have to forget about playing basketball. "Larry" had to get a job, or find another lawyer. He and his mother desperately wanted me to take the case. They had first hand experience with my reputation as a well-respected criminal defense attorney because I had gotten some of "Larry's" cousins off in drug cases. He then asked me how he could get a job, because jobs are scarce. I told him that jobs are scarce only to people who are *not* looking for work; and that if he looked for work every available hour that he wasn't in school or studying, that he would find a job. He came into my office wearing baggy jeans, sneakers and braided hair. I told him to get a haircut, wear a suit and tie. I would not take his case unless he agreed to my conditions.

Larry" was charged with a class "B" felony. If he was convicted as charged he would have been sentenced to a minimum of two to six years in jail, even though he had no prior criminal record. He faced a maximum of 8 1/3 to 25 years in jail. When we went to court, the judge was impressed by "Larry's" appearance. He even asked him where he got the suit. "Larry" explained that it was a high school graduation present. I had a meeting with the prosecutor and judge and they decided to give him a second chance. "Larry" was placed in a pre-trial diversion program, where he received counseling, and his progress in school was monitored. He completed the program and the charges against him were dismissed.

Not every kid I represent is willing to take my advice like "Larry" did. Too many young men are absorbed into a culture of drug-dealing, gang-banging and making babies. Over seventy percent of African-American families are now headed by a single female. What happens to the children? There is a strong correlation between being raised in a single parent household and having an arrest record. Single mothers cannot earn a good living and keep an eye on their children at the same time.

What is wrong with our young men? Why do so many of them think that the only way out of the 'hood' is by dealing drugs or being a rapper? I was fortunate enough to be raised in a family that gave me an understanding of the meaning of hard work. My mother worked the night shift in a factory for seven years until she was hired as a customer service representative at the telephone company. My father always worked two jobs until he was permanently injured in a job-related incident. He was a firefighter, and also owned a window-cleaning and janitorial business. When my brother, sister and I were in grade school, we started working for our father, washing windows, cleaning floors and scrubbing toilets. My father did not pay us for working for him. When we asked for pay, he asked if we ate that day.

When I was seventeen, I got tired of working for my father for free. I needed money. I got a job at Kentucky Fried Chicken and made $1.30 an hour. I worked forty hours my first week and took home forty dollars. When I told my father that I wasn't making enough money at KFC, he didn't feel sorry for me. He told me to do like he did, and get a second job. I took his advice, and before summer was over, I had earned enough to buy my first car.

As I grew older, I was unemployed for brief periods of time. My definition of brief is two weeks. According to my father, "If a person is not working, then he has eight hours a day, six days a week, to find a job." Following my father's advice, it never took me more than two weeks to find a job.

If we are going to save our African-American youth, we need to instill in them morality and a work ethic. A man is not a man if he does not work. A man is not a man if he makes babies with a woman he is not married to. A woman is not a woman if she is involved with a man who is less than a man.

I was in Federal Court on a major drug conspiracy case involving over twenty Defendants. One of the defendants was a major drug dealer whose reputation I was familiar with. The dealer asked the judge to assign him a public defender. In order to determine whether or not the drug dealer qualified for a taxpayer-paid lawyer, the judge asked him questions about his financial situation and the number of children he had. I was shocked to hear that the forty-year old drug dealer told the judge that he had fathered *twenty-six* children. I also learned that one of his sons was a Defendant in the same case.

As a Defense attorney, I risk being accused of being politically incorrect. However, the man who fathered twenty-six children is a menace to the African-American community as a whole. If he is convicted in the drug conspiracy he was indicted for, he should never see the light of day.

It seems that every time I go to a barbershop in a major city, someone comes in selling stolen merchandise. Customers in the shop line up to purchase the "hot" goods at a discount price. The people who buy the stolen goods don't take time to think that the VCR or camcorder they just purchased may have been stolen from a neighbor or friend in a burglary. The hot clothes that they buy were taken from a mall that increases their prices to pass that loss on to the consumer. The person who sells the stolen merchandise is a drug abuser and will give the money that they "earn" in the barber shop to a drug dealer in exchange for more drugs. The drug dealer may buy a gun that will eventually be used to take the life of a young African-American man.

In every African-American neighborhood, there is a red light district. Young women parade around half-naked, selling their bodies to men twice their age to obtain money for their drug habits and to feed their children. Rap music and videos make the lifestyle of "Pimps," "Ho's," and "Bitches" acceptable.

If we are going to save the next generation, we cannot allow the media and recording industry to glorify pimps and whores. Parents need to monitor the music that their children purchase and listen to. The media, music and videos affect the behavior of young men and women.

I recently represented a young African-American suburban male accused of robbery. He and his suburban friends went to a festival in the city and spent the day listening to "gangsta" rap. At the end of the day, they discussed robbing someone. They headed home on the subway; and when they got off the subway, they saw an Asian college student riding a bike. A few of the teenagers that my client was with forcibly robbed the student of his bicycle. My client watched the incident, but did not actively participate in the robbery; he was arrested anyway. His family hired me and I was able to get the charges dismissed. I am convinced that this incident would not have taken place had it not been for the influence of the music they had been listening to that day. I told my client that his mistake was not acting like a leader and preventing the robbery.

My wife is a third grade teacher. We agree that there is a generation of crack babies entering our school systems. Some of these children are classified as "slow learners"; others as "learning disabled"; and some as having "behavioral disorders" or "ADD" (Attention Deficit Disorder). Many of these children entering the school system do not know who their fathers are; some of them were fathered by a "trick".

Some of our children have lost hope. They are brought into this world by parents who are incapable of raising them properly, and live in a community that makes no effort to assist them. I defended one such young African-American man who was sixteen years old, and accused of murder. When I spoke to him, he showed no remorse for the killing of a friend in a squabble over ten dollars worth of crack. When I told him he could possibly go to jail for life, he coldly told me that he was not afraid to die and wasn't afraid to spend the rest of his life in jail.

When I drive through urban neighborhoods, I see the death of our young people glorified on the sides of abandoned buildings with graffiti reading "R.I.P." For every R.I.P. marking the execution site of a young African-American, there is usually another young African-American who bears the responsibility for the killing. This is also an African-American family grieving for the senseless killing of a loved one.

I recall the cries of a woman who came to me pleading for me to do something to save the life of her son who was being hunted down by killers. She explained to me that she tried to raise her son "Mikey" the best that she could. He attended private schools, and became a high-ranking Boy Scout until drugs changed his direction in life. She hired me to defend him in a stolen car case, but was more concerned that a street gang was trying to kill him because of a street fight he had won.

"Mikey" told me that he had dropped out of school. He was depressed because of his parents' divorce; and he had begun smoking marijuana. His habit caused him to become lazy and lose ambition. Every day, he had to cut through backyards because he was being shot at; several times he heard the distinct sound of bullets whizzing past his head. "Mikey" and his mother had reported the incidents to the police; but nothing happened.

I got "Mikey" into a court-supervised drug counseling program and got the criminal charges dismissed. I then introduced "Mikey" and his mother to a tough guy in his mid-twenties, named "Ronald," who I had previously represented for shooting two people, one of whom sustained a very serious wound. "Ronald" was grateful that I was able to work out a deal and served nine months in prison. "Ronald" had turned his life around by the time of our meeting; he had a good job and was married. He was respected and feared on the streets; and knew the gang that was after "Mikey". "Ronald" felt that he could peacefully convince the gang to leave "Mikey" alone.

On the last day of court, "Mikey" and "Ronald" left court together. They went to the neighborhood where the gang targeting "Mikey" hung out. "Ronald" told the gang that "Mikey" was his little brother and it was time to end his dispute. A few weeks later, I received a warm thank-you note from "Mikey's" mother for saving her son's life.

If we are able to re-shape the attitudes of our youth, men from all walks of life need to volunteer their services, time and money to organizations that support youth. For many years, I have coached, refereed, and sponsored young men and women in sports leagues. I have also been involved in mentoring programs. In every one of these organizations there is a need for more volunteers and more money.

I appeal to the adult readers of this book to support the N.A.A.C.P. ACTSO Program, which conducts local and national academic, scientific, and artistic competitions. Join a Big Brother or Big Sister Program. Coach Little League Sports. Become a Boy Scout or Girl Scout Leader. Donate to the UNCF, YMCA or Boys and Girls Club. Support your local chapter of the Urban League. Volunteer at a community center. Take a kid to church.

No one can do everything; but we can each do something.

—John V. Elmore, Esq.

*"It's easier to build strong children
than to repair broken adults."*
—Frederick Douglass

## Appendix A

# Three Criminal Justice System Survivors Tell Their Stories

On November 18, 2003, I interviewed Gail Moore, Billy McCoy and Alfred Houston. All three are recovering drug addicts associated with Group Ministries, a non-profit Christian-based Support Services organization, located on Jefferson Avenue—the heart of Buffalo's Black Community. Their stories follow:

## Gail Moore

*Gail Moore stated that God was the key for overcoming her addiction. She failed several rehabilitation attempts; but none worked until she had a spiritual awakening.*

Gail Moore, a forty-nine year old recovering heroin addict, is a volunteer at Group Ministries, where she leads peer group discussions for recovering addicts. Gail is taking a computer class and is employed at a government agency as an HIV educator. She is a native of Atkinson, North Carolina who moved to Buffalo, New York when she was sixteen years old. It was difficult for Gail to adjust from the slow-paced rural life to the fast urban life in Buffalo; her mother was on welfare and single-handedly raised seven children.

Gail dropped out of school at the age of seventeen. Her peers were into the drug scene; and eventually Gail started smoking marijuana, which made her laugh and feel good. She wanted to keep up with the crowd, and tried other drugs, experimenting with LSD, Tylenol with codeine and other pills. Gail's older brother was a heroin user; she liked to do things that he did. When Gail was twenty, she snorted heroin for the first time; it felt good, and before long, Gail became addicted to heroin.

Gail has been arrested forty times; she shoplifted to support her drug habit. She stole everything from minks, leather coats, expensive suits and other items at shopping malls. She would travel to malls in New Jersey; Albany, New York; Ohio; and other places where she wasn't known, in order to steal. Gail became an expert thief; her targets were small boutique shops; she avoided major department stores where the security was good.

Gail also became involved in prostitution to support her drug habit. She was not a streetwalker. She had several men who would call her and meet her in hotel rooms. Sometimes, she pick-pocketed and stole from her customers. Her clients were older men, both black and white.

The longest time Gail spent in jail was one year. She feels lucky that she was not sent to a state prison that is much harsher than a local jail. She describes jail as a terrible place to be. Women constantly fight over petty things. Holidays are lonely. Some female prison guards are lesbians and make inappropriate advances toward female inmates; there are also problems associated with lesbian inmates. Male prison guards treat female inmates in a degrading manner. Gail described jail as a terrible, sickening, nasty place. The day she got out of jail, she got high on heroin.

Gail feels that she hit rock bottom when her thirty-two year old son came to her apartment and found her strung out on the couch. He also found her needles. She made up her mind that she was going to change. Gail got down on her knees and prayed until she could not cry any longer; she asked God for deliverance from her addiction.

During prayer, she saw a light and believed that God would answer her prayers.

Gail entered a thirty-day inpatient drug rehabilitation program at Sheehan Memorial Hospital in Buffalo, New York. Upon completion of the program, she began participating in Group Ministries, where she got peer support and counseling. She also became a member of Second Chance Ministries where Reverend Arthur Boyd is pastor.

Gail's advice to African-American teenagers is to "understand that there is more to life than drugs, sex and rap music. Do not wait until you are in your late forties to wake up. Women are jewels and should act like jewels. Drugs will make you do things that will endanger your life. Many African-Americans die from overdoses, street violence and AIDS because of the drug culture. Stay away from it. My brother and many of my friends died from AIDS, hepatitis, or overdosed."

## Billy McCoy

*Billy McCoy wants to stop young African-American men from hurting each other with violence and crack cocaine. Billy's message to these young men is to go to college. Older African-American men must step up and help out the younger men. Too many African-American boys are raised by women.*

Billy McCoy is fifty-eight years old. He was born in Birmingham, Alabama where he attended a Baptist Church every Sunday. Birmingham was a segregated city; African-Americans had to sit in the back of the bus and could not eat at white-owned restaurants.

Billy's father had a good job with the railroad company. His family was financially better off than most African-Americans in the neighborhood. Billy recalled being the envy of his peers because his family had the first black and white television set.

In 1952, a white insurance salesman came to the McCoy house to collect on a bill; he demanded sex from Billy's mother and she

153

stabbed him with a knife. Fearing retaliation from the Ku Klux Klan, the family got his mother out of town that evening; she stayed in Tuxedo Heights, Alabama.

Fortunately, Billy's father got a transfer from the railroad to Louisville, Kentucky; and he moved his family there. The family lived in Louisville until the railroad laid off Mr. McCoy, forcing him to relocate to Buffalo where there were other relatives and a strong possibility of landing a job in the steel mills.

Billy was twelve when he arrived in Buffalo. He recalled getting off the train and seeing snow fall for the first time in his life. The family moved to Jefferson Avenue, where they lived with an aunt in a single family home. Eventually the McCoys moved into a rented apartment.

Urban life was new to Billy; he was a country boy who was now exposed to a fast-paced urban life. Billy experienced street gangs and hustlers for the first time in his life.

Billy was a naturally gifted athlete; he was a "Three Sport All-Star" selection in basketball, baseball and football. After graduation, Billy had several scholarship offers for sports, including: North Carolina AT & T and Johnson L. Smith University.

The former Three Sport All-Star remembered that his father spent little time with him as a youth; he could not remember his father ever spending the day with him or taking him places. Instead Mr. McCoy spent his free time hanging out with his buddies. Billy was raised by his mother and aunts.

Despite having numerous scholarship offers, Billy decided not to go to college. Steel factories were hiring; and they paid good money. While working at Republic Steel, Billy made older friends who smoked marijuana; he joined them. Billy also drank wine and hung out in clubs. His uncle owned a bar and gave him a part-time job. *Billy had lots of money.*

One of Billy's friends used heroin. For an entire year, he tried to get Billy to try it. Eventually, Billy gave in. The first time he tried heroin, Billy mainlined (injected the drug directly into a vein).

Billy said that the first heroin high was the most peaceful euphoric feeling that he had ever felt; he liked it from that day on. For the next thirty plus years, Billy was a heroin addict.

Drug addiction caused Billy to lose his jobs at the steel plant and with his uncle. When his mother found out he used drugs, Billy was sent down South to be with his grandmother. The recovering addict described heroin withdrawal as an unbearable painful experience. He suffered from intense headaches, stomachaches, dizziness and cold sweats.

After a year in Birmingham, Billy moved back to Buffalo; he immediately got hooked on drugs again. His addiction continued for over thirty years.

Billy has been clean for eight months. He is a participant in Group Ministries. After going through rehabilitation programs unsuccessfully fifteen times, Billy truly believes that he is in recovery because he found God. Billy said that previously he was spiritually dead. He spent a lifetime chasing heroin to duplicate his first "high". Now, instead of chasing heroin, he chases God.

Billy has been married twice; he has no contact with his children. His daughter is a teacher in Houston, Texas; his son is a crack addict and the father of nine children. As a child, Billy vowed to be a real father, if he had children. He is disappointed at the type of father he turned out to be.

Billy now lives with his eighty-year-old mother; she has taken care of him most of her life. He will now take care of her until she dies. Billy doesn't date or have a girlfriend; he says women reject him when they learn that he still lives with his mother.

Now that Billy has found God, he finally has peace in his life. He is no longer a walking dead person; he is trying to get his life together.

## Alfred Houston

*Alfred Houston feels that members of the African-American community tolerate drug dealers. He said that African-Americans should cooperate with the police and have the dealers put away so that they do not infect the entire community.*

Alfred Houston is sixty-three years old. He is college educated and holds a master's degree. Presently, Alfred is an administrator at group Ministries. He is also a deacon at Second Chance Ministries.

Alfred's life wasn't always as stable as it is now. In the 1970's, he was a pimp, known as the "Black Mariah". He had girls working for him in New York City, Buffalo, Toronto and Halifax (Canada). In the 1980's, Alfred was a superintendent of a large housing project on Lenox Avenue in Harlem (New York). He also ran a drug operation in the basement of the project, which employed up to twenty dealers; and at its peak, earned twenty-five to thirty thousand dollars a day.

Alfred has served prison time in a federal penitentiary in Lewisburg, Pennsylvania, a prison in Wisconsin and a prison in Canada. He is a recovering crack addict.

After living life on the edge, Alfred has found peace through Christ. He wants to warn the next generation about the dangers of crack cocaine. Alfred stated: "No drug known to mankind is as dangerous as crack; it will make housewives come out of nice homes and become "Crack Whores". Crack turns grown men into violent predators, and is responsible for the destruction of black communities."

According to Alfred, "If crack is legalized, we will lose this country." He is in favor of stronger penalties for crack cocaine than powder cocaine because crack is more powerful and more destructive.

*"I have a dream that my four little children will one day live in a nation where they will not be judged by the color of their skin but by the content of their character."*

—Reverend Dr. Martin Luther King, Jr.

## Appendix B
# The Perils of Being Black In America—Let the Truth Be Told

In many instances Being Black in America, may have be all that's required to propel you into the criminal justice system. For centuries, the discrimination and cruelty instigated by racist law enforcers toward African-Americans have caused death and destruction to thousands of defendants, their families and even their neighbors. To give you a sense of the historic significance, I've recapped a few of America's most publicized African-American trials.

## Historic African-American Trials
(Source: *Great American Trials—200 Compelling Courtroom Dramas* and *http://search.eb.com/blackhistory*)

### The "Great Negro Plot" Trial of 1741 (New York, Colony of New York)
Most cases during the 18th Century have been untold; but because of the vast circumstances of this case, it has become documented as a part of American history.

In 1741, a panic was started over a so-called "plot" involving a conspiracy that would create an uprising among slaves to burn New York and murder its white citizens. It all began when a few isolated incidents occurred involving burglary by two slaves, a white tavern owner who dealt in stolen goods, and a series of fires, which involved theft and arson supposedly started by two other slaves. In addition to the exaggerated testimony of several frightened defendants and a very frightened 16-year old slave girl who claimed that her master (the tavern owner) held meetings with large groups of slaves that talked of burning the town, the prosecutor presented the legally inadmissible testimony of a convicted thief.

This was an example of false testimony used by and against the defendants of a criminal trial, who were falsely accused of conspiracy (agreeing to commit a crime). No lawyer in New York would agree to defend the accused, which resulted in "guilty" verdicts for 106 of the 170 defendants named in the case. The verdicts included 23 death sentences: sixteen black and four white defendants were hanged; thirteen black defendants were burned at the stake. In addition, seventy blacks and seven whites were banished from British North America.

## State of Missouri Vs Celia, A Slave (1855)

Even though the law stated that it was forbidden to take any woman against her will and by force, enslaved women had no legal recourse when their masters raped them. Celia, a nineteen-year old slave had two children by her master who had purchased her when she was fourteen. Her master raped her and continued to force himself upon her for five years until she became compelled to stop him; Celia had even asked his daughters to intervene and discourage him from demanding sex.

One last time, amid her un-availed pleas to stop, Celia killed her master with two blows to the head by a heavy stick. She burned the body, but later confessed. Even though Missouri law states "a homicide committed while warding off such a crime (of rape) was justifiable" Celia was found guilty of murder in the first degree and sentenced to hang by the neck until dead.

Although a defense attorney, had represented Celia in the 19th Century, Blacks were not allowed to testify in criminal trials, so she had to give statements to the prosecutors to read at the trial.

*One of the questions that occurred was whether the rape statute embraced slave women as well as free white women, because slave women were considered "property" of their masters.*

## Huey P. Newton Trial (1968) Oakland, CA

Huey P. Newton was one of many African-Americans who were profiled by the police and the criminal justice system. He was an illiterate high-school graduate, who taught himself how to read before attending Merritt College in Oakland and the San Francisco School of Law. He later received a Ph.D. in social philosophy from the University of California at Santa Cruz.

In 1966 Huey Newton and Bobby Seale, who had met at the San Francisco School of Law formed the Black Panther Group. The group's purpose was to find ways to counteract incidents of alleged police brutality and racism and to demonstrate the need for black self-reliance. *By the late 1960s, the party had grown to 2,000 members in chapters that spanned several cities.*

With the Panther's growth came many conflicts between Black Panthers and the police, which resulted in shoot-outs in California, New York, and Chicago. In 1968, within a year of founding the Black Panther Group, Newton was convicted of voluntary manslaughter in the death of a police officer. Just short of serving two years in prison, however, he was released because of an overturned conviction.

In 1971 the Black Panthers adopted a nonviolent manifesto and dedicated itself to providing social services to the black community.

Although the Panthers had turned from violence to concentrate on conventional politics and on providing social services in black neighborhoods, its members had been targeted as "threats" to the white system and would have no peace from the law. They were subjected to police harassment that sometimes took the form of violent attacks and false accusations.

Huey Newton was accused of another murder in 1974; but two trials for the crime resulted in hung juries. In 1978, he was sentenced to a six-month jail term for misappropriating public funds intended for a Panther-founded Oakland school; later that year Huey Newton was found shot dead on a street in Oakland.

## Hurricane Carter (1966) Trenton, NJ

Far too many African-Americans have been unjustly arrested and/or tried in criminal court just because they were "born black in America". Hurricane Carter was one of those men.

When he was a child, Carter intervened as a local political figure attempted to molest one of his friends; this act was met with a vengeance and continued harassment by the police, which did not stop until they put Carter behind bars.

In 1966 Ruben "Hurricane" Carter was the number-one-ranked contender for the middleweight boxing crown when he and a companion were arrested and charged with the murders of three white people. Based on fraudulent evidence, illegal evidence and faulty identifications, they were convicted and narrowly escaped the death penalty. Carter was sent to Trenton State Prison and later to Rahway.

While in prison, he wrote the story of his life, *The 16th Round: From Number 1 Contender to Number 45472* (1974), which ultimately saved his life. His impending rescue began in 1980, when Lesra Martin, a 16-year-old African-American youth from Brooklyn purchased a copy of Carter's book for $1 while in Toronto, Canada at a used-book fair. After reading the book, Martin convinced his Canadian friends that Carter was innocent; and together they set out to help him gain his freedom.

After several rejections by the New Jersey courts, a United States District Judge held in 1985 that the prosecution had withheld critical exculpatory evidence and improperly argued racial hatred as the motive for the crime. *Habeas corpus* relief was granted and after 20 years of unjust incarceration, Carter was released from prison.

Unfortunately, there is no program in place for restitution; and given his successful career as a professional boxer, it could be conceived that Carter's unjust incarceration caused him to lose millions of dollars in income revenue.

There is no better example of the importance and value of the Writ of *Habeas Corpus* than the case of Rubin "Hurricane" Carter, who was freed by a federal judge after being wrongfully imprisoned by New Jersey for almost 20 years. In spite of his being locked up for two decades, Rubin Carter has surfaced as one of the most eloquent spokesmen in support of the Writ of *Habeas Corpus*. He has testified before Congress, spoken at law schools; and is the director of an international organization (the Association in Defense of the Wrongly Convicted),

## Angela Davis (1966) Los Angeles, CA

Professor Angela Y. Davis is known internationally for her ongoing work to combat all forms of oppression in the U.S. and abroad. Over the years, she has been active as a student, teacher, writer, scholar, and organizer; she is a living witness to the historical struggles of the contemporary era.

Davis' political activism began as a youth in Birmingham, Alabama. In 1969 she came to national attention after being removed from her teaching position at UCLA as a result of her social activism and her membership in the Communist Party, USA.

In 1970, she was placed on the FBI's Ten Most Wanted List on false charges, and was the subject of an intense police search that drove her underground and culminated in one of the most famous trials in recent history. A massive international "Free Angela Davis" campaign led to her acquittal in 1972. Harnessing the momentum of that campaign, she co-founded the National Alliance Against Racism and Political Repression, which continues its work today.

Professor Davis has lectured in all 50 states, as well as in Africa, Europe, the Caribbean and the former Soviet Union. She is author of five books including *"Angela Davis: An Autobiography"* and *"Women, Race and Class"*.

# Appendix C
# Names & Numbers That Will Help You Win The Fight For Your Life

The resources below have been created to assist you or someone you know. If you have been arrested, accused of a crime or incarcerated, it is imperative that you understand your rights. These organizations and agencies have information that can help you win the "*Fight For Your Life*":

## Attorneys:

**Keith Branch**
**Executive Director**
Nat'l Assoc of Blacks in Criminal Justice
NC Central Univ - P.O. Box 19788
Durham, NC 27707
(919) 683-1801
www.nabch.org

NABCJ is designed to serve the needs of African-Americans and people of color at all levels, including nonprofessionals, paraprofessionals, and professionals. Anyone can become a member of the Association. The National Association of Blacks in Criminal Justice encourages ex-offenders to join and contribute their perspectives to this unique and dynamic organization.

**National Association of Criminal Defense Lawyers (NACDL)**
1150 18th St., NW, Suite 950
Washington, DC 20036
(202) 872-8600          Fax (202) 872-8690
assist@nacdl.org

The National Association of Criminal Defense Lawyers (NACDL) is the preeminent organization in the United States advancing the mission of the nation's criminal defense lawyers to ensure justice and due process for persons accused of crime or other misconduct. A professional bar association founded in 1958, NACDL's more than 10,000 direct members—and 79 state and local affiliate organizations with another 28,000 members—include private criminal defense lawyers, public defenders, active U.S. military defense counsel, law professors and judges committed to preserving fairness within America's criminal justice system.

**The Foundation for Criminal Justice**
1150 18th St., NW, Suite 950
Washington, DC 20036
(202) 872-8600                     Fax (202) 872-8690
assist@nacdl.org

The Foundation for Criminal Justice is the independent charitable organization of the National Association of Criminal Defense Lawyers. It supports fundamental fairness in the criminal justice system. It advances the promise and protection of the Bill of Rights, including the right to be free from unreasonable search and seizure, the right to due process, and the right to effective assistance of counsel.

## Crime Victims:

**National Center for Victims of Crime**
2000 M Street NW, Suite 480
Washington, DC 20036
Phone: 202-467-8700                Fax: 202-467-8701
Website: www.nvc.org               Hotline: 800-FYI-CALL

The National Center for Victims of Crime is the nation's leading resource and advocacy organization for crime victims. Since 1985, they have worked with more than 10,000 grassroots organizations and criminal justice agencies serving millions of crime victims to help them rebuild their lives. NCV offers crime victims, victim service providers, criminal justice officials, attorneys and concerned individuals practical information on the closest, most appropriate local services for victims of crime.

## Domestic Violence:

**National Coalition Against Domestic Violence**
P.O. Box 18749
Denver, CO 80218
Phone: 303-839-1852/Hotline: 800-799-SAFE (7233)/Fax: 303-831-9251
**(If you need immediate assistance, dial 911)**

National Coalition Against Domestic Violence (NCADV) was formally organized in January 1978 when over 100 battered women's advocates from all parts of the nation attended the U.S. Commission on Civil Rights hearing on battered women in Washington, DC, hoping to address common problems these programs usually faced in isolation. Today, NCADV remains the only national organization of grassroots shelter and service programs for battered women.

## Alcohol & Drug Addiction:

**Alcoholics Anonymous**
P.O. Box 459
New York, NY 10163
Phone: 212-870-3400
Website: http: alcoholics-anonymous.com
In the U.S./Canada: Look for "Alcoholics Anonymous" in any telephone directory.

Alcoholics Anonymous (A.A.) is a fellowship of men and women who share their experience, strength and hope with each other that they may solve their common problem and help others to recover from alcoholism.

The only requirement for membership is a desire to stop drinking. There are no dues or fees for A.A. membership; they are self-supporting through their own contributions. A.A. is not allied with any sect, denomination, politics, organization or institution; does not wish to engage in any controversy; neither endorses nor opposes any causes. Their primary purpose is to stay sober and help other alcoholics to achieve sobriety.

**Cocaine Anonymous**
3740 Overland Ave., Suite C
Los Angeles, CA 90034-6337
Hotline: 1-800-347-8998 24hrs
Phone: 310-559-5833        Fax: 310-559-2554
E-mail: cawso@ca.org        Website: www.ca.org

Cocaine Anonymous (CA) is a national program of recovery, which was adapted from the program developed by Alcoholics Anonymous in 1935. Like AA (with which they are not affiliated), CA uses the Twelve Step recovery method, which involves service to others as a path towards recovery from addiction. Cocaine Anonymous is open to all persons who state a desire to stop using cocaine, including "crack" cocaine, as well as all other mind-altering substances. There are no dues or fees for membership.

## Police Misconduct:
**American Civil Liberties Union**
125 Broad Street
New York, NY 10004
Website: www.aclu.org

Since their founding in 1920, the nonprofit, nonpartisan ACLU has grown from a roomful of civil liberties activists to an organization of nearly 400,000 members and supporters, with offices in almost every state. The ACLU's mission is to fight civil liberties violations wherever and whenever they occur. Most of their clients are ordinary people who have experienced an injustice and have decided to fight back.

## Sexual Abuse Helpline Resources:
**Rape, Abuse, Incest National Network (RAINN)**
635-B Pennsylvania Avenue SE
Washington, DC 20003
Hotline: 1-800-656-HOPE (4673)
E-Mail: RAINN@aol.com
Website: www.rainn.com

The **Rape, Abuse and Incest National Network (RAINN)** is a non-profit organization based in Washington, D.C. that operates a national toll-free hotline for victims of sexual assault. Founded by singer/songwriter Tori Amos (who is herself a rape survivor) and funded with initial grants from the Atlantic Group and the Warner Music Group, RAINN began operating in 1994. In cooperation with 865 rape crisis centers across the country, RAINN offers confidential crisis counseling, for survivors of sexual assault who cannot reach a rape crisis center through a local call, or those who might not know that a local center exists.

**Voices in Action**
8041 Hosbrook, Suite 236
Cincinnati, Ohio 45236
1-800-7-VOICE-8 (1-800-786-4238)
E:mail:voicesinaction@aol.com
Website: www.voices-action.org

Voices in Action is an international organization providing assistance through educational programs to adult victims of child sexual abuse. They help victims become survivors and create accurate public awareness of the prevalence of child sexual abuse, its impact, and ways in which it can be prevented or stopped.

# Index

# ORDER FORM

## WWW.AMBERBOOKS.COM
### African-American Self Help and Career Books

Fax Orders: 480-283-0991
Telephone Orders: 480-460-1660
Online Orders: E-mail: Amberbks@aol.com

Postal Orders: Send Checks & Money Orders to:
Amber Books Publishing
1334 E. Chandler Blvd., Suite 5-D67
Phoenix, AZ 85048

_____ *Fighting for Your Life*
_____ *The House that Jack Built*
_____ *Langhorn & Mary: A 19th American Century Love Story*
_____ *The African-American Woman's Guide to Great Sex, Happiness, & Marital Bliss*
_____ *The Afrocentric Bride: A Style Guide*
_____ *Beautiful Black Hair: A Step-by-Step Instructional Guide*
_____ *How to Get Rich When You Ain't Got Nothing*
_____ *The African-American Job Seeker's Guide to Successful Employment*
_____ *The African-American Travel Guide*
_____ *Suge Knight: The Rise, Fall, and Rise of Death Row Records*
_____ *The African-American Teenagers Guide to Personal Growth, Health, Safety, Sex and Survival*
_____ *Aaliyah—An R&B Princess in Words and Pictures*
_____ *Wake Up and Smell the Dollars! Whose Inner City is This Anyway?*
_____ *How to Own and Operate Your Home Day Care Business Successfully Without Going Nuts!*
_____ *The African-American Woman's Guide to Successful Make-up and Skin Care*
_____ *How to Play the Sports Recruiting Game and Get an Athletic Scholarship:*
_____ *Is Modeling for You? The Handbook and Guide for the Young Aspiring Black Model*

Name:_____

Company Name:_____

Address:_____

City:_____State:_____Zip:_____

Telephone: (_____) _____E-mail:_____

For Bulk Rates Call: **480-460-1660**          # ORDER NOW

| | | |
|---|---|---|
| Fighting for Your Life | $14.95 | |
| The House That Jack Built | $16.95 | ❏ Check ❏ Money Order ❏ Cashiers Check |
| Langhorn & Mary | $25.95 | ❏ Credit Card: ❏ MC ❏ Visa ❏ Amex ❏ Discover |
| Great Sex | $14.95 | |
| The Afrocentric Bride | $16.95 | |
| Beautiful Black Hair | $16.95 | CC#_____ |
| How to Get Rich | $14.95 | |
| Job Seeker's Guide | $14.95 | Expiration Date:_____ |
| Travel Guide | $14.95 | **Payable to:** |
| Suge Knight | $21.95 | Amber Books |
| Teenagers Guide | $19.95 | 1334 E. Chandler Blvd., Suite 5-D67 |
| Aaliyah | $10.95 | Phoenix, AZ 85048 |
| Wake Up & Smell the Dollars | $18.95 | |
| Home Day Care | $12.95 | **Shipping:**    $5.00 per book. Allow 7 days for delivery. |
| Successful Make-up | $14.95 | **Sales Tax:** Add 7.05% to books shipped to Arizona addresses. |
| Sports Recruiting: | $12.95 | |
| Modeling: | $14.95 | **Total enclosed: $_____** |

John Elmore is a practicing criminal defense attorney with offices in Buffalo and Niagara Falls, New York. Mr. Elmore is a former New York State Trooper, Manhattan District Attorney and New York State Assistant Attorney General.